A PRACTICAL GUIDE TO CREDIT AND COLLECTION

A PRACTICAL GUIDE TO CREDIT AND COLLECTION

Successful Techniques to:
- Implement a Systematic Program
- Improve Cash Flow
- Build Customer Loyalty

George O. Bancroft

amacom
American Management Association

Library of Congress Cataloging-in-Publication Data

Bancroft, George O.
    A practical guide to credit and collection : successful techniques
to implement a systematic program, improve cash flow, build
customer loyalty / George O. Bancroft.
        p.   cm.
    Includes index.
    ISBN 0-8144-5953-6
    1. Collection of accounts.   I. Title.
HG3752.5.B36   1989
658.8'8—dc19   88-83151
                                                                   CIP

Printing number

10   9   8   7   6   5   4   3   2   1

CONTENTS

PREFACE

IN TODAY'S business environment cash flow is the lifeblood of any company. A sad but true fact is that the front line guardians who control, to a great extent, this lifeblood, have little or no training in the strategies and procedures that keep the flow moving.

These are the people who handle accounts receivable credit evaluation, collection of delinquent accounts, and file maintenance. In many instances they are left to their own resources in developing an adequate program that delivers the needed cash flow.

This book is written directly to, and for, that person who covers the front lines of defense against the lack of funds that many companies are feeling today. It presents a detailed program about everything you ever wanted to know about credit and collections (well, almost everything). It can also be used very effectively by the experienced credit executive as a tutorial for new employees. I might go so far as to say that many seasoned credit managers may be surprised at the morsels they pick up by reading through the book.

This is a people-oriented program because the business arena is populated with people who must interact in a better manner so all can be more productive and more profitable. It stresses that delinquent accounts are still customers, and that they should be rehabilitated if at all possible—thus bringing in good, promptly paid business in the future.

The program presents a well-planned approach to the increase of cash flow. It insists that the collectors are not just responsible for collecting delinquent accounts receivable, which stimulates current cash flow, but are also one of your company's most important influences on current receivables and, most of all, future sales.

The program starts with the groundwork and builds a solid structure that allows those who use it to review any accounts receivable program—within any company—with total confidence that they have the tools they need to "clean it up" and institute a program that will keep things running smoothly from that point on.

The role of the collector is a high-level, professional position that industry in general has failed to acknowledge. Not just this country, but the entire global commercial community now runs on a "foundation of credit." Take away this crucial element of commerce and the world's economy would crumble.

This book introduces tools for the collector that have never been presented before—such as the psychology of the collection situation, and the most effective telephone collection program ever used. It also presents a detailed chapter on the steps you can take to analyze your current credit and collection program, and to start immediately building a strong well-structured program that will "bring in the bucks"—because when it comes down to the bottom line, that's what it's all about.

Chapters 7 through 10 provide you with a complete credit and collection procedures manual to use "as is," or as a guide to establishing your own set of company credit and collection procedures.

The main emphasis of this book is on the strategies and hands-on techniques for your credit and collection department, whether it be a hundred people running a program on a large mainframe computer, or a single person in a small company that needs help in organizing the company program. The book works for both situations and all you folks in-between.

There are areas that are not covered here. These areas were left out on purpose, generally because they each deserve an entire book to cover the topic adequately, and those books do exist. Here are some of the topics which I do not cover, or at least not in much detail:

Commercial law: This is a complex area that has been covered for many years by *Credit Manual of Commercial Laws,* compiled by the National Association of Credit Management.

Financial analysis: This, too, is complex and requires a full-length book. I recommend *Financial Analysis: Tools and Concepts,* by Jerry A. Viscione.

International credit and collection laws: This area is so complex and so extensive that it takes more than one book. If your company is heavily involved in international credit and collections, I recommend investing in *Digest of Commercial Laws of the World,* by Lester Nelson.

These books are published by the National Association of Credit Management, 520 Eighth Avenue, New York, N.Y. 10018–6571.

I would like to extend my warmest appreciation to Jerry Eyland, John Hampton, David Hennekes, and Jack Edelstein for their help in reviewing my manuscript, and for sharing their expertise and for making valuable suggestions that have made this book more valuable to you, the reader.

A PRACTICAL
GUIDE TO
CREDIT AND
COLLECTION

Chapter 1

MODERN MYTHS OF THE CREDIT INDUSTRY

I<small>N THIS</small> chapter you discover the true role of both the debtor and the collector. You see what your relationship, as the collector, should be to the vast majority of your company's customers. We will give you insights that will change your perception of the role of the collector, and as you start changing your perception, your actions will also change. In doing this, many of your debtors may unknowingly also change their character in dealing with you.

We'll explore your real role in your company, because you can literally make or break your company by the way

1

you do your job. You'll discover some interesting facts about the sales department. It has people working for it that you wouldn't guess in your wildest dreams. I think you're going to be surprised.

Are there days you end up putting back the pieces when sales or the order desk or the billing department or some other employee has dropped the ball? We have the answer you have been waiting for. It's one of the most important things that you need to know to love your job—and do great work.

Myth #1: The World is Full of Individuals Who Want to Cheat You Out of Everything They Owe You

First, let's admit that there are people out there who are doing their best to cheat companies out of products, services, and money. We must also realize that there are other people who put off paying their bills, for no good reason, until the bills become long overdue. But such people are in the minority, and by using proper procedures, you can identify and handle this minority.

The small group of people who set out to "rip off" anyone and everyone they can get to often includes their own customers as well as creditors. For years this type of person used the protection offered by the corporation laws, in an attempt to dodge financial responsibilities. But in recent years our legal system has attempted to deal with such obvious abuses of consumer rights and responsibilities—as best it could.

We are now seeing many courts "pierce the veil" of corporate protection, allowing creditors to deal directly in some cases with officers and directors of bankrupt corporations. Corporate responsibility has become the watchword. Directors of corporations have been put on notice that they can, and will, be held personally responsible for both the proper and the improper conduct of their corporations. This problem has grown to such an extent that corporate directors can now buy liability insurance to protect themselves.

There is another type of rip-off artist who plagues the American business community. This is the consumer who buys with no intention of paying anything more than a small down payment, if that. This type of person typically feels that society owes him or her as good a standard of living as possible.

But you must remember one thing. A person does not simply wake up one morning and say, "Society owes me; I'm going to start taking." Debtors of this type usually have a poor payment record and a history of instability.

Even if a person is young and has no payment history, there are still ways of identifying signs of instability, and therefore ways of protecting against substantial losses. These are discussed in Chapter 4, "Making the Credit Decision."

It can't be stressed strongly enough that these two examples of irresponsible individuals represent a very small percentage of all delinquent debtors. Most delinquent customers have a reason for not paying. The reasons vary, but I have found that in many cases they are caused as much by the creditor as by the debtor.

In dealing with delinquent customers, you must approach each collection situation as if there were a valid reason for the customer's not paying. Your primary function, as the collector, is to identify this problem and present a workable solution that is agreeable to both your company and the customer.

Myth #2: Whatever I Have to Do to Collect My Company's Money Is Right Because the Debtor Owes Us the Money

After working in the front line of the collection field for a number of years a person can become cynical and negative about the whole collection situation. After all, this person has dealt with nothing but the company's problem customers all these years, and the collector can actually begin to think of all customers in the same light. Many of them face "burnout"—I know—I've been there! When all you see and hear day after day are problem accounts, it can become a real emotional drain.

With the laws as tight as they are, many collectors become frustrated in their attempts to collect what is genuinely owed to their company. This is accentuated in companies where collectors have quotas or delinquency percentage limits that they must meet month after month, that stretch the abilities of even the best collectors.

This is the point when some collectors begin to feel that whatever measures they take to collect the money are justified.

Another situation where you find the "we're right" syndrome is where a company has no consistent collection policy or no ongoing effective collection program. Suddenly, someone in top management realizes that the company is short on cash—and he or she realizes that too much money is tied up in receivables. The word goes out to the collection department, "Clean up that mess; use whatever means you have to . . . we need the money."

The problem here is that the customers have been left to "pay as they see fit" for months, and now they are hit with a "pay up or else" attitude from a surly collector who has suddenly had the screws put to him or her, and the company ends up losing what may have been a group of very profitable accounts—and the sales department is wondering why its accounts won't talk to it anymore.

If anyone doubts that this type of collector doesn't exist in today's world, you are wrong. I recently met one of these folks. Even with canceled checks, he wouldn't believe that I had paid my bill, and continued to send me nasty notes. The shame is that this company has the best product in town, but I am now a customer of their competition. When you have a strong, consistent collection program running smoothly, month after month, you will not have to rely on this type of collection tactic.

The point is that you, as the collector, can't do "whatever it takes" to collect the money. You must do it within the laws of the land, and more than that, you *should* do it with dignity and a human touch.

Myth #3: You Have to Be Hard-Nosed and Abusive to Be an Effective Collector

There are two main contributors to the birth of the heavy-handed collector. The first is the situation described in Myth #2. This attitude demonstrates a complete lack of understanding, on the creditor's part, of *what* the credit/collection function should be. The second contributor is a complete lack of adequate training for credit/collection personnel. Most collectors have little or no practical training and simply end up learning as they go.

There have been some training programs, but most are concerned more with laws, and tactics for asserting the creditor's rights to the maximum without landing in legal hot water.

Because the laws governing credit were so slanted toward the creditor's side during the first half of the credit industry's growth period, little emphasis was placed on handling people properly. Techniques for handling debtors became more and more heavy-handed and abusive. The arrogant, overbearing collectors who could intimidate debtors into paying were collecting more than those with no program at all, and therefore, became the models for the industry.

With no alternatives available, new people entering the credit field as collectors continued to use and develop techniques based on the old hard-nosed approach. One harassment technique led to another and aggravated the situation until the government stepped in with laws that gave debtors some rights of their own, however belatedly. Companies then issued policy statements proclaiming "Fair Treatment to All Customers," in some cases even issuing procedures manuals and training manuals that supported the new policy statements.

But the policy statements, procedures manuals, and training materials still had one major shortcoming. While presenting the *what* and *why* of these new policies and procedures, they left out the *how.* Again, no alternative. So the hard-nosed, abusive collection tactics simply went underground. They are still there and are still being used actively. Their form may have changed somewhat, but the underlying philosophy that guided their growth has *not* changed. Why? Because no one provided a workable alternative.

In the highly regulated world of today's credit industry, you are still left with a closet full of unusable techniques and tactics, and nothing to replace them. As a result, you may feel as many collectors do, that your job is next to impossible.

Because a new day is dawning for the credit industry, a new approach *must* be taken, and it *can* be taken far more effectively than before. This book gives you a totally new, fresh approach that will bring in the cash and retain the customer as a friend, and future source of business for your company.

Myth #4: If the Customers Don't Like the Way We Handle Our Collections, Let Them Go Somewhere Else—We Don't Need Delinquent Accounts

I think you will agree that it is easy to see how this kind of thinking can become common among collectors. Many collectors see the delinquent customer as an undesirable that the company can easily do without. In reality, most debtors whose accounts become past due are embarrassed by their delinquency. At the same time, because collectors have reputations as hard, uncompromising professional intimidators, debtors know they can expect no understanding and/or sympathy. So they attempt to avoid a confrontation. Their attempts to avoid a humiliating situation lead you to assume the debtor is trying to avoid payment.

By the time you finally talk to the debtor, the actual situation is blown far out of proportion in both of your minds. Thus it becomes a never-ending spiral of hostility—extremely nonproductive for both the customer and your company.

Many potentially good customers who have found themselves, for one reason or another, in this kind of situation have declared they will never do business with that company again. And you may say, "Good-bye and good riddance." But wait, your company might have just lost thousands of dollars in good, solid future business. This doesn't seem like a sensible way to run a business, but it still happens all the time.

Myth #5: The Credit and Collection Administrator Position Can Be Handled by an "Entry-Level" Employee

Is *this* myth way off base!

The role you play in the total operations of your company has been grossly misunderstood over the last four decades. Because top management has had little regard for your true role, and the many contributions of a well-run credit and collection program, little emphasis has been placed on your training, upgrading your credit and collection skills, and your job level.

Both the credit investigator, and the collector have very responsible positions that, if done inefficiently, or in a loose and sloppy manner, can cost your company thousands of dollars.

As shown in Myth #3, your job may even be looked down on by other employees in your company because of misunderstandings. This image is completely false, of course, but how do you go about changing things if you face this dilemma? You are on the right track right now. The philosophies and procedures described to you in this book can allow you to upgrade your department, and the view that other employees have of it—and you. In the next chapter I give you some of the methods that I have used in the past to remedy this very type of situation.

Both you and the company president must acknowledge the true importance of the credit and collection department. In the next chapter you are given a cash flow diagram that places you, the collector, in a crucial position in the cash flow of the company. I will prove that you are responsible for generating a major share of the company's available, spendable cash.

Regardless of the reason your company needs additional money, it may spend additional sums in interest on the borrowed money, if the receivables are not collected on time. With a well-trained, motivated employee following the procedures in the program presented in this book, the company may not need to spend the extra money on interest for borrowed money.

Myth #6: The Sales Department and the Credit/Collection Department Can Never Work Together Because the Sales Representative and the Collector Have Different Goals

First and foremost, you must be a member of the sales team. A healthy collection program is one that motivates the customer to pay. You are a *salesperson* competing against other creditors for "first available money." You are a part of the sales team because no sale is truly complete until the product or service has been paid for.

The sales department and the credit/collection department must become aware of their true relationship. You each represent one step in a continuous process. Neither is more important than the other in the long run. Any time your two departments are not working closely with each other for a common cause, the company loses.

A well-run, positively motivated collection department can be one of your company's strongest sales tools. All company personnel who deal directly with customers are basically salespeople. Your collection department holds an especially sensitive position in the cash cycle because of its unique relationship to the customer.

You are not just responsible for collecting delinquent accounts receivable—you are responsible for stimulating (or impeding) an increase in cash flow. You can influence not only delinquent accounts but also current receivables and, most of all, future sales.

Myth #7: A Good Part of the Collector's Time Is Wasted Solving the Problems Created by the Blunders of Other People

Your job is filled with problems, most of them caused by other people. This is a fact that you must face early on. But this fact should not lead to a distorted view of your position in the company, or your importance to the business. You are not wasting your time when you are solving problems created by others.

For example, members of the sales team may constantly do things that seem to make your job harder. Every day in the United States, thousands of billing errors and "special payment" deals are traced directly to the sales department. Thousands of times a day, all across the country, merchandise that has been returned to the salesperson for credit is finally discovered under the seat or in the trunk of his or her car.

For one reason or another, the salesperson may send the customer an order "without charge," without notifying the billing department of these special terms; this becomes a problem and it is your job to step in and straighten up the mess.

What you may fail to realize is that the gift of the $100 "error" may have saved an account of $100,000 per year for the company. It is easy to become disillusioned when dealing in such situations and you only have some of the relevant facts at hand.

Communications are essential in all aspects of business. Without communicating, you cannot do a good job or maintain a healthy attitude. It is simply too easy to become bogged down by constant contact with delinquent customers and other peoples' errors.

The collection department sits at the hub of a very important circle of activity. You *must* know why things are done and what effects they may have on business. You must also understand and appreciate the fact that people are human and therefore prone to mistakes.

In the business community, you must solve many problems caused by human error, simple neglect, and other factors that you should not only accept as a fact of life but welcome as an opportunity to test your skills. You are the professional problem solver. Look at that as a positive aspect of your job. It is your mark of distinction. When you see it as an important role, and when you do it with a smile, your fellow employees will start seeing you as their fellow professional and not the ill-tempered "clerk" in accounts receivable.

Myth #8: Send Them the Bill—If It's Wrong, the Customer Will Let Us Know— It Doesn't Matter Anyway

One of the major problems each collector faces is the prevalence of invalid billing. And all too often, no one else in the company seems to care. In this one area, small businesses with unsophisticated accounting and billing systems, and large companies sporting the latest in computer technology, share the same problems.

Sometimes it seems that the people in the company accounting and billing departments consider themselves and/ or their computer infallible. The truth is that today's computers rarely make mistakes. But they *are* typically filled with mistakes because *people* feed them information.

If your company has a history of billing errors, you must never assume the validity of any information shown on a customer account file. All collection activity should be approached as though an error might be possible. You should then verify the information and double-check *before* beginning any collection activity, especially in dealing with long-delinquent accounts that have had little collection activity.

As a corollary, processing credit memos, debit memos, and other file adjustments must all be part of your constant, ongoing, updating program. An accounts receivable file that is clogged with invalid billing only slows you down in performing your main task (collecting *delinquent* money) and will, at the same time, give you, and your company a negative image.

When a company relies on its customers to find the billing problems, it is paying too much for the service. Invalid billing that is allowed to reach a past due status wastes processing time in sending invalid past due notices, collector time in nonproductive work, and customer goodwill.

An accounts receivable file maintenance program must be started and followed regularly to stop this waste of time and money, and halt the erosion of customer relations.

Myth #9: It Doesn't Matter Who You Call First—You're Going to Call Them All Anyway

It is essential to establish and follow a collection program that is both cost effective and efficient. Too often collectors follow a program that assumes all past due customers will be contacted *sometime* during the month. They have no priorities in terms of who should be called first, or how the contact should be made.

They don't consider who should be called on the telephone, who should receive a letter, or who needs a personal visit. One of the major factors, so often overlooked in establishing the typical "priorities-by-default" system, is account dollar value.

In the collection business, *dollars collected* is the name of the game. Any other priority is a false one. And yet, month after month, collectors give the same priority to $100 delinquent accounts and $10,000 delinquent accounts. To be the most effective collector possible, you must establish priorities for the types of accounts that require the various methods of collection, and the sequences for contacting the customers.

When the old myth prevails, "We're going to contact them all, so let's start at the beginning," the company loses. All delinquent accounts are not equal, and even if they were, those at the end of the alphabet are rarely given equal attention.

In Chapter 5, "Establishing a Well-Structured Collection Program," I describe the method that you can use to determine which accounts are sent letters, which accounts are called, and the priority of the calls, and why and when you make a personal visit to a customer site.

Myth #10: The Best Delinquency Percentage Is Zero Percent

When a company takes all the credit business available and still has no accounts receivable delinquency—that's great. But it never happens in the real world.

During a particularly bad day (or days) you may begin to feel sorry for yourself and decide the company should take only Grade A Prime business. This type of thinking has two fatal flaws built in.

First, if there were no past due accounts, there would be no need for you or your collection program. Each company takes certain risk accounts knowing that a percentage of them will go past due, but collectors are hired to control the situation. No delinquency—no jobs.

Second, very few companies offering credit take all the credit business they can get. Management must make initial policies as to how potential credit customers will be judged and what the guidelines will be for acceptance or rejection.

Other judgments must be made as to the dollar amount of credit that will be extended in each case. If a company takes only prime credit risks, it will cut out a large number of accounts that might generate a huge profit over the years.

Setting parameters that will bring as much *profitable* business as possible, without simultaneously sending the delinquency rate sky-high, is an important function in any well-integrated credit/collection program.

In Chapter 4, "Making the Credit Decision," you learn a set of guidelines that you can use for your credit investigation and credit decisions.

Chapter 2

THE RULES FOR SUCCESS

In AREAS such as science and mathematics we all accept the rules, or laws, as the structure around which we can build and explore. Even in areas as ambiguous as psychology there are certain rules that the profession, or at least parts of the profession, accept as laws that must be followed in all practical applications.

The area of credit and collection is no exception. There are rules that act as laws of action and reaction. When the six basic rules discussed in this section are followed, you the collector, immediately become more productive. It doesn't matter if you work in the collection office of a manufacturer, for a bank, or as the person responsible for

15

collecting delinquent accounts for a doctor or dentist, these rules will work for you.

I have taken these tested, proven rules of success, and applied them to the accounts receivable department.

Try 'em—you'll like 'em.

Rule #1:   Become a Salesperson

You are an important part of the sales team. That much you should understand up front. This may seem to be a contradiction of everything you have been told about your role in the company, but it is a fact. While most credit/collection departments have no direct reporting lines to sales or marketing departments, they are involved in very important segments of the sales cycle.

Your Role in the Buying Decision

First, the credit/collection department gets involved at the time of the "buying decision" by providing the means for closing the sale. The salesperson may have brought the customer to the point of commitment, but without the O.K. of the credit department the sale cannot be truly closed.

It is important that you understand your role here. The credit decision is a critical part of the sale, and the way it is handled is important. Many sales have been lost simply because the credit check took too long or was done in a less-than-professional manner.

When you enter the picture, the salesperson has brought the customer to a point of commitment. This commitment seems to be to buy your company's product. That is what a sale appears to be on the surface. But a commitment to buy on the part of a customer is far deeper and more meaningful than that. A commitment to buy is a commitment to *action*.

Once a customer makes the mental decision to move, or to act, they usually wish to start—immediately. A slow credit check can lose the sale. The customer is intent on moving—in this case, buying—and if *you* act too slowly, they will move on—to the competition.

You must bring a sense of urgency, and a proper sense of its importance to the task. You must realize that you, as a member of the credit department, can make or break the sale.

This is not to suggest that sloppy or hasty procedures should be acceptable. You must always perform a thorough credit check, looking into all aspects carefully. But, if the process will take longer than usual, make a quick call to the sales department or to the customer, if appropriate, to relieve any tension and protect the sale.

Remember—communication is the key!

Your Role in the "Back End" of the Sales Situation

The second main task of the credit/collection department, that of collecting past due accounts, is also an important part of the sales cycle. A sale is never completed until the bill is paid-in-full. The sales department can sell ten times its assigned quota, but until the customers pay the account in full, the company has only *lost* money.

You are always in a very sensitive position during the collection sequence. The methods and tactics used to collect past due accounts not only reflect on the current month's cash flow, but on cash flow and profits for years to come. The way you handle your customers will determine whether or not they will ever buy from your company again. You must use a subtle mixture of psychology and sales engineering to motivate the delinquent account to pay you and love doing it.

Remember, you are part of the sales team—always! It is so easy to fall into the "good guys—bad guys" syndrome that permeates the American business community. Some companies are so departmentalized that each little "feudal kingdom" views the other departments as the enemy.

This antagonism is very prominent between sales departments and credit/collection departments. Each sees the other as having different goals. The antagonism becomes even worse when the separate departments work in different physical locations, because it is much easier to dislike someone you don't know or seldom see.

Again, I return to one of the essential ingredients in a smooth, well-run organization—communications! Communication is the key. If you find yourself in a situation in which sales and credit are not working together, you must make the effort to break down the walls yourself. Attend a sales meeting. Get to know the salespeople by name. You may even want to make some joint calls with them to become better acquainted with their operating methods.

In any case, don't become a party to departmentalization and polarization. All of that is nonproductive for you and for the company.

Rule #2:   Understand Your True Place in the Company

Your company's ability to pay its bills, develop new products, build new facilities, and expand its position in the marketplace is in your hands. You have a great deal of responsibility and occupy a high-level position. You directly control the cash flow of your company because you control one of its major assets—the receivables file.

Evaluating a Company's Net Worth

This book is not intended to present a complete evaluation of financial statements, but I thought it might be worthwhile to quickly cover two of the financial documents the accountants use to assess the financial condition of a company. These two documents are the balance sheet and the income statement.

A complete explanation of these statements is not rel-evant in this discussion. To pinpoint the real role of accounts receivable in your company's financial condition, a short overview of these documents in needed—zeroing in on the areas that are affected by accounts receivable collections.

BALANCE SHEET. The balance sheet shows the worth of the company at a particular place in time. It divides the financial aspects of the business into two major categories. The first of these is assets. Assets are all the items that the company owns or has an interest in that have a dollar value.

The other category is liabilities, which includes all the financial obligations the company has. Accountants subtract liabilities from assets to determine the company's net worth.

Assets. The asset side of the balance sheet is broken down into smaller categories.

- *Current assets*—those items that can be most easily converted into spendable cash. These include:
  —*Cash*—considered the most liquid commodity in the current assets group. Of the five main cate-gories of current assets, only cash is used as working capital. It is in the bank and available for immediate use. The main source of replenishment is from receivables.
  —*Stocks and bonds*—also very liquid; that is, they can be cashed in and used to pay bills with relative ease. However, stocks and bonds are purchased as investments, and though they are there for emer-gencies, they are not generally used to generate working capital.
  —*Prepayments*—payments made to items such as rent and utilities that would have required the use of operating cash through the next accounting period (until the next balance sheet is made up). Because the company does not have to make the payment

in the next accounting period, it carries the amount as an asset through that period.

—*Receivables*—debts owed *to* the company which can be converted to cash in the bank. The condition of the receivables file is the true indicator of the validity of the amount listed as a current asset on the balance sheet. You are directly responsible for the condition of the receivables file—that is, the actual *collectibility* of the dollar amount shown. This means that you, the collector, are responsible for a very important company asset.

—*Materials and inventories*—also available for sale in an emergency, but they are not there for that purpose. Inventory is maintained to provide materials for producing the products to sell and does not by itself generate cash flow.

* *Long-term investments*—the next area of assets on the balance sheet. These are investments that are carried for net worth value. They rarely become a factor in the daily operation of the company.

* *Property and equipment*—the last items in the assets category on the balance sheet. They represent the buildings owned by the company and the large equipment items that generally have a value over $500. These assets are generally depreciated over a long term, such as five to fifteen years for equipment and twenty to thirty years for buildings.

Liabilities. The liabilities side of the balance sheet is also broken down into smaller parts.

* *Current liabilities* are generally those items that must be paid within a year. These are:
  —*Accounts payable*—generally the trade accounts that your company buys from on a regular basis. These are due on a monthly basis.

—*Notes payable*—the short-term notes that the company may have taken from its bank or any other source of working capital. These are not open accounts like the accounts payable, but are generally a loan for a specific reason.

—*Accrued liabilities*—such items as wages that have accrued for vacations, FICA payments to be sent to the government, and taxes that have accrued.

—*Advances by customers*—such as down payments that are paid before delivery.

—*Current portion of long-term debt*—sometimes reflected in the current liabilities.

* *Long-term liabilities*—can be divided into the following types of categories:

  —*Bonds payable*—corporate bonds that have been sold for a particular project, and have a long-term maturity.

  —*Mortgages*—also long-term debts, with the exception of the current year's payments.

  —*Other long-term liabilities*—can consist of outstanding contracts, pension plan payments, as examples.

These are general accounts that a company may use to produce a snapshot of its financial health at a particular point in time.

The difference between the assets and the liabilities is the net worth, or owner's equity. The owner may be a person or group of people. If the company is a corporation, this is called the stockholder's equity.

INCOME STATEMENT. The other major financial document is the income statement which is compiled to show the company's profit or loss during a specified period.

The income statement shows

* Gross sales revenue
* Returns and discounts

• Expenses incurred against revenue
• The final profit or loss figure

The final profit or loss figure on the income statement is converted to an account on the balance sheet. The perfect situation might be that the company's profit for the month is 100 percent in cash. This means that each month the profits would go directly into the bank.

One of the places that profit can go on the balance sheet is to accounts receivable. When this is the case, it is possible for a company to show a healthy profit month after month and still go broke, because they are unable to collect what is due them.

Selling products at a profit does not necessarily mean the company will prosper and grow. The missing ingredient is working capital, which can easily be tied up in receivables. It is possible for a company to "sell" itself into insolvency.

The cash cycle. To get a clearer picture of this, let's look at a typical business cash cycle (see Figure 1).

Available Cash

Before any business can open its doors it must have a certain amount of spendable cash, which is provided by . . .

Owners, Investors, or a Bank

Available cash to start a business and support it through the first stages usually comes from one or more of three sources. The owners put up the capital from their own resources, or they find other people with available cash to invest, or they borrow the money, to be spent for . . .

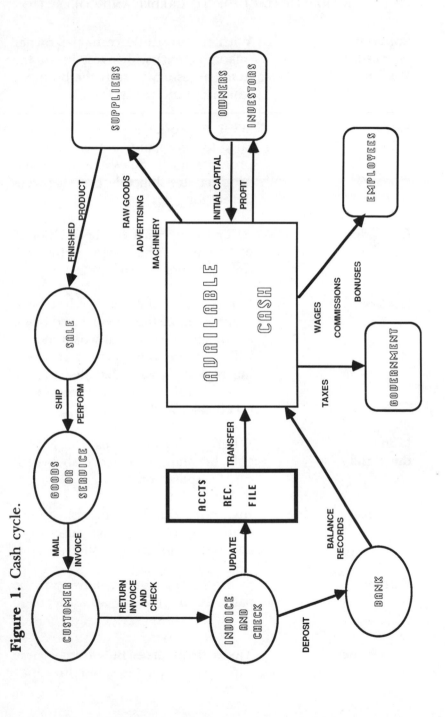

Figure 1. Cash cycle.

Supplies, Inventories, Facilities	With the available cash, the owner (management) will invest in all the items necessary to start the business, which is now ready for . . .
Sales	With a product/service ready for sale, the company can go out and promote itself. Sales are made and products are shipped or services rendered for . . .
Customers	After the product has been shipped or the service has been performed, the customer is sent an . . .
Invoice	Up to this point money has been spent to make the product and bring about the sale, without which money will continue to be spent until working capital is totally depleted. At the time of sale, the item becomes a receivable, and . . .
Money in the Bank	When the invoice is paid, a receivable becomes available cash, which can be spent for . . .
Supplies	Inventory can be replenished, operating supplies can be purchased, and payments can be made to . . .
Employees	Salaries and commissions can be paid. Payments will also be made to . . .
Government	Taxes, taxes, taxes! But after all these expenses are paid it is time to repay the . . .

Investors	The people who get paid last are those who most deserve to be paid, because without them there would have been no . . .
Available Cash	But wait! What if the customer doesn't pay? That means no available cash and the company either borrows, finds more investors, or ceases operations. *You* are the key!

Your Role in the Company

Your job is of top-level importance, and so are you. You control the cash flow of your company. Balance sheets and income statements are valuable, and show the relative health of your company, but they don't tell the whole story. Profits must be translated into cash flow. The sale must be completed. You are the final stop in the sales circle.

You have close contact with the problem accounts of your company, and your ability to find adequate, workable solutions is critical. The manner in which you handle those problem accounts not only reflects on the current delinquency rate but on future sales.

At all times you must act like a professional. Your role is the same as the professional salesperson's. You must be businesslike but personable. You must sell yourself first, and you must never be high and mighty or heavy-handed in your approach to customers, even to those who openly challenge your ability and position as a collector. There are legal methods for handling the true problems, and if you get emotionally caught up in the collection situation, you will impair your productivity.

Always remember . . .

Your job is made up of problems. Most of them are caused by other people. *Accept this as fact!* The company has hired you to handle those problems and those situations. It's your job. Approach each situation as if you were the answer—you are.

Rule #3: Know Your Company

As a credit/collection administrator, one of the most important things you must know is the company you work for. You must know its organizational structure, its people, its products, and its policies.

You must know who does what, when, why, and how. Few other positions have the close contact with so many different facets of the company.

Know the Organization

If you are not completely familiar with the structure of your company and its people, you should make an organizational chart of the company and fill in name, position (title), duties, and telephone numbers for all department heads. If you work for a small company, it may not be necessary to draw an organizational chart. But if your company is large enough to warrant your preparing the chart, I guarantee it will make you more effective.

If you can pick up the phone and call *the* person you need, you'll save time, and when you think enough of that person to call him or her by name, the response to you will be made in a more positive manner. Try it—it works.

Know the People

As you prepare your organizational chart, filling in the names and getting to know the people, watch for indications of your department's place in the hierarchy.

Answer the following questions:

- How are you looked upon by your company peers?
- Do people act kindly toward you or is there a sign of hostility now and then?

- Is the hostility everywhere?
- Are you treated with apathy ("You don't get no respect")?

This is not a book on interpersonal relationships, but for the sake of your effectiveness within your company, I would like to review the role of organizational politics in job effectiveness. *Remember—nice is better . . . ALWAYS.*

Enter every situation in an understated manner. Don't be the meek soul who never stands up, but remember how difficult it is to "put down" someone who attempts to be decent to you.

I know it works—I've tried it!

I worked in a situation once where my department was considered the "dregs" of the company. I found it impossible to get my job done because everyone disliked the department and its people, and refused to cooperate. Unfortunately, their attitude was justified—my fellow workers in the department were less than likable. They were hostile and abusive to everyone, from habit.

But I needed to get my job done, so I spent time making friends with people in various departments within the company. Soon they knew me as a person and not as part of a group they disliked as a whole. I was able to do the job and ended up becoming the manager of the department.

Making friends always works—it's communications in action.

Know the Product

Your company's product is as important to you as the organization's people. You cannot be truly effective as a credit/collection administrator until you have a thorough knowledge of your company's product line.

This means knowing all products sold and all of the accessories. You must know their names and the model numbers. You must also know prices. If you have more than one price list, you must know them all—and who uses which ones—and why.

In your attempt to be the most effective credit/collection administrator, you must know one more thing about your company and its product—you must understand what your company's *real product* is. This may sound a little strange, but it really isn't if you give the matter some thought.

Most companies sell a product that can be at least defined and specified in writing. It may be as tangible as a truck or as nebulous as consulting services, but in all cases if you were to ask an old pro on the sales team what the company sells, you might be surprised at the answer.

Good salespeople sell results. That is, they sell answers to a desire or a problem. Once you understand what your company really sells, you will be in a much stronger position to deal with delinquent customers. You will be able to continue to sell results.

WHAT WAS THE REAL PRODUCT? Let me give you an example of what I mean about identifying your real product. During the twenties, thirties, and forties, many motion picture empires were built. Today few of those studios are still around. What happened?

At the end of World War II, television appeared. This phenomenon broke many of these motion picture studios because they had not properly identified their product. Those who did survived, and those who have emerged since the 1950s understand the true role of the motion picture studio. These studios grew during a time when their peers were "going down the tube."

Most studios saw their product as films to be shown in theaters around the country. They perceived television as a major threat to their industry and fought against it. Those who survived saw television as a possible source of revenue for films of certain types. While they produced films for TV, they continued to produce films that were "bigger" than television, or not suitable for the television audience for any number of reasons. They avoided direct competition and concentrated on separate segments of the market.

I mention all this to demonstrate that you should not assume your product to be what is only obvious on the surface. Give it some thought. Once you have zeroed in on the true product, credit decisions and collection activities will be much easier, because you will know why your delinquent customers buy your company's product. When you know the main reason they buy, you can approach your collection efforts from their viewpoint. This will make you far more effective in your collection activities.

You must also determine your company's position in the marketplace. You should know:

- Your place in the market. Are you strong or weak, and why?
- How long your company has been in business. Is it an old established firm, or a new "up-and-coming" one.
- Who the market leaders are by name and what your company's position is by comparison. Maybe you are the leader.

Knowing who you are within your company, and knowing who your company is in the business community, will help make you a professional. Take the time to find out. It will pay off time and again in your credit/collection activities.

Know Where Your Department Fits

Once you have identified your place in the company and your company's position in the marketplace, and have learned about the product line, you must turn your attention inward to your own department. Find out the following information:

- What are company credit policies?
- Are they written down in a procedures manual?
- Can you get a copy of the written procedures?
- Will your manager go over the procedures with you and explain them?

Look around and learn about your company, its people, and its product before looking at your own department. Department policies and procedures—the "how" and "what"—are often shaped by the "who" and "why."

The who and why are usually found outside your department. The policies and procedures used in a company are generally the result of who the company is, and what it sells.

It is possible to write policies and procedures that are general enough to be applicable to a wide range of situations, but basically those would be rules written within a vacuum.

This book contains the "what" and the "how" for twenty-five credit/collection department procedures, but probably no two companies will put this manual into practice in quite the same manner. To a great extent your company is a product of its industry, and of its place in the industry.

**Know the Company Policies
and Procedures**

You must be aware that general company policies, and the policies and procedures of the other departments within the company, have a direct effect on the implementation of your credit and collection policies and procedures.

If your company has not seen the need to establish written procedures for the credit/collection department, carefully review Chapters 7 through 10 in this book and use these as a guideline for your own policies and procedures. You will probably wish to change some of the items, adding explicit instructions that apply to your company.

The final word on policies and procedures is to be sure that they apply to your unique situation, and that they have the support of all related parties.

THERE MAY BE "UNWRITTEN RULES." Along the same line as written policies and procedures are the rules that are not written down, but are understood by everyone involved. These might include the rules governing deals that are made on payment plans.

Most delinquent customers find it impossible to bring their accounts up-to-date with one payment. This means payment plans must be worked out.

Some companies have strict rules that govern who can approve payment plans, while others give the collector a free hand. You have to know about these unwritten rules and how they are applied, if they exist. It's essential to know—so ask your manager.

Know the Collection Program

You must also know the collection cycle intimately. You must know who gets statements, collection notices, collection letters, when they get them, and how often they are mailed out.

THE NOTICE / LETTER CYCLE. The first thing to memorize is the notice and letter cycle. Know who gets delinquent notices and when they are sent, and by whom. They may be your responsibility. You should know:

- The number of notices and letters in the cycle
- The intervals between each notice or letter
- The text of each notice and each letter
- The special accounts that do not get notices under any circumstances—and why

- The alternative collection procedures used for the accounts that don't get notices or letters

If you are going to call a past due customer today it would be helpful to know that a past due notice was sent yesterday. If you resolve the delinquency situation, you can then tell the customer to disregard the notice in the mail. This will probably avoid irritation and save a good customer.

THE TELEPHONE PROGRAM. Next, learn about the telephone collection program, if your company has one. Learn the following:

- The number of calls you are expected to make in a day, in a week, in a month. Find out if there is a measurement.
- Do customers who get telephone calls also get notices or letters? If so—when? How many? Which ones?

PERSONAL VISITS. Personal visits to the customer's business location or home was the normal collection procedure in the past. During the last two decades, many companies replaced field collections with telephone collections and found the phone as effective and far less expensive. While a field collector can make ten to twenty calls a day, a telephone collector can make fifty to seventy or more calls—with the same success percentage.

There are, however, times when a field call is necessary. Find out who will make such calls. In your company, the person may be someone already in the field, such as a sales representative or a service person, or it may be you. Better find out.

BADLY DELINQUENT ACCOUNTS. Procedures for handling badly delinquent accounts are sometimes very general. You should know:

- Whose responsibility it is to send the letter placing the customer on COD.
- At what point in the collection cycle the letter is sent.
- If there is a written COD list, or some other flagging system in use, you should determine:
  —What it is.
  —How the account is flagged.
  —Who is responsible for doing it.
- What happens after the COD letter is sent. A typical COD letter gives the customer a period of time (5 days, 10 days, 2 weeks) to pay before he or she actually becomes a COD customer.
- What the follow-up procedure is and who is responsible for it. Again, find out what your responsibility is.

OUTSIDE COLLECTION SERVICES. Most companies use an outside collection service of some kind to handle the final action on very delinquent accounts that cannot be resolved by company personnel. This may be an attorney, for legal action and follow-up collection, or it may be a separate collection agency. You should find out:

- The agency or attorney to use
- When to use the outside source
- What procedure to use in assigning an account
- What procedures to use for following up on the outside service

WRITE-OFFS. Last, learn the procedure for writing off an account. A write-off may be a concession that management has decided to give the customer, or it may be a bad debt that is not collectible. If you have any responsibilities in these areas, learn the procedures.

Your Goals and Objectives

Let's talk about one more item concerning you and your relationship to the credit/collection department—your job goals and objectives. The only way to get the recognition you deserve for a job well done is to define what you are going to do before you do it.

Because each situation is different—and continually changing—it is impossible for me to set down a list of goals and objectives that you can follow. You and your manager must do this. Write your goals down and identify the tasks to be done, and give each one a priority rating.

Write specific goals and objectives, using dates and percentages and/or dollar figures where possible.

Example:

- By July 31, 19XX, total delinquency over 30 days will be reduced to 20 percent of the total outstanding.
- By July 31, 19XX, 90-day delinquency will be reduced to 5 percent of the total outstanding.
- During fiscal year 19XX, bad debt write-off dollars will be less than .1 percent of the total billed for the year.

These are simple and very general objectives, but they give you the idea. Include specific points in your objectives that fit your situation.

Rule #4: Know Your Accounts Receivable File

To be an efficient, effective collector, obviously you must be familiar with the accounts receivable file system your company uses. Here are some of the areas you need to learn.

Storage Media

Your company probably uses one of the following methods for storing the accounts receivable information about its customers.

**Statement
Cards**

Statement cards are generally small-to-medium-size forms, printed on paper or card stock, used to physically record each transaction for each customer. Every payment, every charge, and every credit or other adjustment must be entered by hand onto the card.

This process is only as dependable as the people using it. It is usually not kept up-to-date on an hourly or daily basis. This type of system is generally used by smaller companies. Manually posting all entries is one of the major drawbacks of the system.

**Small
Business
Computer**

That "timing" problem can be overcome if you are fortunate enough to have a small computer system at your immediate disposal. If all records are stored on a small in-house computer, and if all collectors and other personnel who work with the file have instant access via separate terminals, every transaction can be recorded as it occurs. In this way each account is always completely up-to-date, which makes your job as a collector much easier. It eliminates anxiety—no system is perfect, but you can be reasonably certain that when you call a customer regarding an overdue balance you are using correct, current information.

Service Bureau

If your company uses a service bureau, you probably work with a series of printouts from last week or a couple of days ago. It is important that you update this account information daily so that your customer payment date is as current and relevant as possible.

In-House Mainframe Computer System

A large computer system that requires a special computer room is called a mainframe. This type of system is generally the best type to work with, if the system has been programmed within the last ten years. This means that the most current real-time programming techniques were most likely used and you have accurate accounting data at your disposal when making collection calls.

Even if your company does have its own in-house large computer system, you may still be required to use a batch system, which may not be ideal, but still guarantees reasonably current records. A batch system is one where all entries for the day are made at the same time, in one batch. This is generally done on the second or third shift.

Whichever type of account storage system your company uses, you must know your company's system, what kind of records you are asked to work from, and their comparative accuracy.

Those actual records may take one of several forms. You may work from invoices taken from an invoice tub

where all current invoices and/or past due invoices are kept
to be taken and "worked" at random by various collectors.

The same type of system may be used, but the invoice
tub may be, instead, a statement tub. Or, you may work
directly from a computer printout that lists all past due
accounts together with all the information you should need
to make calls or send notices.

Some companies use combinations of the above, while
others use systems entirely of their own devising. Usually
specific accounts are assigned to specific collectors. I believe
the individual assignment system is preferable because it
allows each collector to become familiar with a specific group
of customers, and thereby promotes accuracy and understanding.

Know your company's system. Trace the routing of
each type of sale from the moment of sale to the actual
collection "tool" you hold in your hand when you contact
the customer for collection. Look for areas of possible error
and learn to check in those areas before you assume accuracy, especially before you challenge a customer.

The Update Cycles

You must know how often the collection document you
work with is updated. This information will come with your
understanding of your company's accounts receivable system. For example, if you use an in-house computer and
everyone in your department has regular access to it, accounts should be updated constantly and should always
contain current information.

But if you use a service bureau or batch system, accounts may contain information a day or two older, and
therefore they may not be accurate. If a delinquent customer
makes a payment on Tuesday morning, you may not learn
of it until Wednesday. If you call for collection on Tuesday
afternoon, and you assume complete accuracy in your file,
you may embarrass yourself and your company.

Sometimes this lag time is much longer. Computers have cut it down tremendously; before the computer age, accounts were often updated on weekly, biweekly, and even monthly cycles, which practically guaranteed inaccurate information on the file. It still happens, but with much less regularity.

Equally important, you must know how old the updating is when you learn of it. If it is instantaneous, you have complete control, and that's nice. But if it is done at night, do you know about it the next morning? If you use a computer service, your system probably works that way.

But remember, if transactions are billed by hand, you may not see the new information until it is several days old.

THE ACTUAL UPDATING. Is there one person assigned the job of updating the receivables file, or is each collector responsible for updating his or her own records?

How are you notified when updates occur? If your company gathers all such transactions and completes them in daily or weekly batches, you should know the system that is used to notify you of the changes in the accounts.

YOUR UPDATING METHODS. You need a simple, consistent method to update your own working file. The system should help you keep track of changes, updates, and other relevant activities, so that you know you're working with the most current information.

If you deal with dozens of accounts, in situations involving hundreds of individual transactions, the only way to survive is to be simple and consistent. This is true because computer printouts, delinquent lists, updates, invoices, statements, and other forms reach your desk in a ceaseless flood.

Assume your company uses a service bureau, which provides you with a monthly listing of all your accounts. The listing includes such information as payments made, last purchase, delinquent balance, and length of delinquency.

You also receive a daily update that includes all payments, adjustments, credits, and purchases from the previous day.

First, you always work with the most current listing of all your accounts and their status. As soon as you receive each new monthly listing you would work through it account by account, identifying (perhaps in colored ink) all the 90-day plus delinquencies for immediate collection.

Within half a working day you will have gone through the listing item by item and circled, underlined, and otherwise marked all of the information relating to companies and accounts that you intend to deal with first.

Every morning, as soon as you receive your update, take the listing and transfer all of the update information onto your working file before making any calls, or sending any letters. Never work with old information, even if it is only a day old, when more current information is available.

You might use a colored ink, or "highlight" system to identify the type of action you are going to take on each account.

SETTING YOUR PRIORITIES. In one company where I worked, we received a monthly account printout that showed all accounts spread as current, 30-day, 60-day, and 90-day-plus invoices. The first thing I would do when I received my status report was to analyze it.

I would then draw a bright red line down each page between the 30-day invoices and the 60-day-plus invoices. The reason is simple. The status report was as of the last working day of the month. By the time I received the status report, all of the invoices in the 60-day column were 90-days old. I then treated all accounts with invoices on the right side of the red line alike.

The next thing I would do was categorize my accounts into collection type. I found that 80 percent of my delinquency was in 20 percent of my accounts. Since my goals had been set to emphasize the collection of *dollars,* I concentrated my personal collection efforts (telephone calls and personal visits) on the big dollar accounts.

I also prioritized my personal calls. The bigger and older the account, the higher on my list of collection activity. We'll cover the whole procedure of setting collection priorities in Chapter 5, "Establishing a Well-Structured Collection Program." You, too, may want to devise a system of your own, or your company may require you to use a standard system for updating that everyone in your department follows and understands. What matters is that you use a consistent system that identifies problem accounts at a glance and guarantees that all up-to-date information is on your record for your use.

Your Update Report

Your company's file update system should include a list of all payments and adjustments made to your accounts the previous day. That is, unless you handle the whole receivables accounting function and post your own payments and adjustments.

If a sales representative authorizes a credit, and fills out a form on the spot, and hands a copy to the customer, how soon will that credit appear on your update report?

There is a good chance that it will not appear at all. This could be one of those transactions that is handled entirely by hand, on a different schedule than the normal update schedule.

WHAT DO ALL THE ENTRIES MEAN? You should understand all of the entries on the listing of updates you are sent by your computer department, or your service bureau. Learn to identify each type of transaction instantly so that you can read the update as though it were written in standard English.

Some of the obvious notations (for example: CR, DB, Pmt) probably do not require an explanation, but it is a good idea to list all of the abbreviations you use and define them so that other people can look at your listing when you are not there, and make sense of your update notations.

Once you understand all of the notation symbols on the update, try tracing an adjustment through the audit trails shown on the report. This may not seem necessary to you at first, but eventually a customer is going to challenge you on a particular piece of information and you will have to be able to trace your own information as soon as possible.

You must know where it came from, who entered it, where they got it. It's all part of the same process—understanding your company and its system. You must understand your own department and the tools provided for you—forward and backward—because as a collector you have to work in both directions sometimes.

THE FILE ADJUSTMENTS. Who actually makes the adjustments to a customer account? You may be lucky and have a computer terminal at your disposal, working on a "real time" system, which means that you can enter the adjustment onto the record exactly as it occurs. But maybe your company uses the batch system, which means that all adjustments are entered by a separate operator, entering data between 6 P.M. and midnight. Whoever it is, you need to know the routine, and the person that does the work.

The person who originates the paperwork for each adjustment is different, depending on your company and the management philosophy. Some companies allow a sales representative to authorize it in the field. Other companies insist that adjustments must be handled only by a certain person assigned to adjustments within a certain department. Some companies require that all adjustments be okayed by an officer of the company. You must know how these situations are handled in your company to be the most effective collector you can be.

KEY CONTACTS. It is a good strategy to have a "key contact" in both the originating department and the computer department (if your company has an in-house computer department, or if you use a service bureau). Get to know the people involved in these areas. Know who is responsible for what, and try to develop a good working relationship with these people so that you can depend on them for answers when you need them.

One day a customer will call with a special request or problem, or you will call a delinquent customer and run into a problem you did not expect. In this situation you need to know the right person to contact to get an immediate answer and clear things up with a minimum of fuss.

Remember, your fellow workers can make things much easier for you if you get to know them and get used to working with them so that you function smoothly as a team.

Again, if all adjustments of a certain type are made by one person, that is, returned parts are credited only by a person in the parts department, or one department, you must be able to go to that person or that department for all your answers. But if adjustments can be made by any number of people, you must know this and also know, by looking at the adjustment, who made it. In this case you will want to cultivate a good relationship with all of them.

Adjustments on the
Customer Account

This refers back to the earlier topic about knowing your company's notation system. When you see an amount with an alphabetic notation beside it, do you understand what the entire entry means? Does $10CR mean a credit of $10 has been given to the customer? You should know any additional information about the adjustment that would lead you back in an unswerving path to the original source document, and ultimately the person originating the adjustment.

ENSURING THAT THE ADJUSTMENT IS MADE. Whether or not your own department is responsible for writing up the actual paperwork for adjustments, you should have some means of seeing that it does get processed and applied to the customer account.

Sometimes you may have to take matters into your own hands when the regular person responsible for adjustments is sick or on vacation. You should know how an adjustment is made under those circumstances. This type of condition will most likely affect your work.

If a customer complains that a $25 credit has not been posted to his or her account, and your checking proves that this is correct, you should know how to get it done so you don't have to sit helpless, and wait, and hope—meanwhile knowing that the customer will not pay a delinquent billing if matters are not cleared up "right now."

POSITIVE ACTION TO AVOID ADJUSTMENT PROBLEMS. It is impossible to lay out an exact program for you to follow when evaluating the adjustment part of the collection program. Companies are too unique and have their own rules that must be followed. But to guard against the possibility of these problem areas causing recurring customer problems and unneeded delinquency, you might consider listing all of the possible problems that might occur in this whole adjustment area. Then you might list possible solutions in each case, so that when the problem occurs (as it almost certainly will someday) you will be ready with the answer. A good way to start such a preventive maintenance program is to:

1. Produce a list of all of the people who are responsible for adjustments of any kind.
2. Cross-index and -reference the list with job functions in such a way that any problem can be plotted against the system and handled in the proper manner.

Such exercises help you develop a comprehensive understanding of your department and your company. After you have done your homework, no situation will come up that will baffle you, and your work will be notable for its consistency and accuracy. This may seem like an awful lot of work—even senseless work—but you and your company will discover that it is worth it in the end.

Checking Billing for Validity

Some day your customer monthly statement will be challenged by a customer. Most of these challenges will be claims of invalid billing. Customers are great for yelling computer error (which is in fact human error blamed on the poor helpless machine), claiming unrecorded adjustments, unshipped goods (they really mean unreceived goods), and so forth.

In all cases, you need to know where to go to get answers. First of all, do not automatically assume your company is right. You must assume that the customer is right until you can absolutely prove otherwise. Even if the customer is wrong, you must handle it in the most diplomatic way you can to keep a happy customer.

If you have done the research I suggested earlier, and answered all the questions we have already asked, you are prepared to deal with claims of invalid billing. You know who, or what department, issues credit memos. You know where the authorization originates, and you know who makes the initial decision even before the authorization is obtained. So you know where to start your search. You know what the source document is. You know how the information is stored, and you are prepared to read any printouts or billing notations that contain the information you need.

But just in case, use Figure 2 to follow the sale through, from the actual customer purchase to the moment of the customer complaint. This form asks the questions that could come up, one at a time.

Delinquency Percentage

Finally, in understanding your accounts receivable file you must learn to deal with delinquency figures—percentages and the like. Make note of the following:

Figure 2. Customer adjustment checklist.

CUSTOMER ADJUSTMENT CHECKLIST

Customer Purchase

1. Where did the customer make the purchase?

☐ Home/office   ☐ At our location ———————————   ☐ On the phone

2. How was the merchandise delivered?

☐ On the spot ☐ By mail ☐ Delivery service ———————————   ☐ By company truck

3. Can we verify delivery to customer?

☐ Delivery receipt   ☐ Signed invoice

Producing the Invoice

Type of invoice   ☐ Handwritten   ☐ Typed   ☐ Computer generated

Who generated the original invoice?   ☐ Outside sales rep ☐ Inside sales clerk ☐ Other ——————

Is one person or dept. responsible for generating invoices? Who? ————————————————

Where was the invoice produced?   ☐ Sales office   ☐ At various sales desks   ☐ Parts, Sevice Dept., etc.

Are invoices prenumbered? ——— Is blank invoice stock under lock? ———Can invoices get lost? ———

Can invoice get processed but order get lost? What controls? ————————————————

Who controls invoice copies? ———————————— How many copies are created? ———

Posting the Invoice

Who posts the invoice ? ———————————— How? ☐ By hand   ☐ By computer program

When does posting occur? ———————————— Chances for error ————————

How soon does invoice show on A/R reports and/or computer program? ————————————

Making an Adjustment to the Invoice

Who makes adjustments? ☐ Anyone who writes an invoice   ☐ Billing dept.   ☐ Credit memo desk only

How are adjustments made? ————————————————————

How and when posted to A/R file? ————————————————

How are you notified? ————How long after adjustment written? ————————————

How do you know if it is valid? ————————————————————

What additional information needed on adjustments? ————————————————

- Most companies divide the delinquent accounts into four categories: 30-day, 60-day, 90-day, 120 days, and over.
- You should know what percentage of your accounts is involved in each of these categories.

• Know the dollar amount involved, and how it relates to the total.

When you know these percentages, you know something of the status of your department, and you have something to measure the department's progress against. At the same time, you should know your own percentages so that you can measure your own performance independently.

PRODUCTIVITY IS THE NAME OF THE GAME. You should locate and be able to name your ten highest dollar accounts in each of the above categories. It is a fact that you will find that 80 percent of your delinquent dollars are tied up in 20 percent of the accounts. By identifying these high-dollar delinquent accounts and successfully collecting them, you can decrease your delinquency figure dramatically. You will also be increasing your company's cash flow at the same time. It is important to remember that not all accounts are equal.

It often takes just as much effort to collect a $10 account as it does to collect a $10,000 account. I can state categorically that it does not take one thousand times more effort to collect the $10,000. Knowing that and putting this knowledge to work will make your collection effort far more productive.

ANALYZE YOUR COLLECTION RESULTS. You should know what the historical trend of delinquency has been in your company, and in the accounts that you are assigned. Sometimes there are regular cycles in the delinquency that you need to be aware of.

There may be certain accounts that always wait 45, 60, or 90 days before making payment. If you find that this is true in your case, work these accounts to try to cultivate a better payment habit. See if you can work with their accounts payable people to improve their payment record and improve your own performance record.

If you deal with large institutions or government agencies, you are sometimes wasting your time trying to alter their payment systems—it might be better for you to alter your billing to accommodate their payment system. Just think about it. You may find that your billing system is the problem.

I once had a government account that was constantly paying late. When I investigated, I was told that the purchase order number was incorrect. It seems that our PO number field had only twelve characters and when a PO number was entered, it would truncate (cut off) any characters over that length. This customer had PO numbers that were in series, all starting with the same numbers. The last numbers were what they needed in order to pay.

To solve the problem I had to have our billing department change the way they entered the PO number, and enter just the last twelve characters. The customer paid on time after that.

There are some occurrences you should look out for. These are sudden unexpected drops or increases in delinquency percentages. If you suddenly have a very low delinquency percentage, it might be because of high current sales. Sometimes delinquent percentages can be falsely lowered because of sudden high sales volume. The reverse is also true. You can have a suddenly high delinquency percentage due only to low sales in the last month.

If your company averages a fairly even $100,000 per month in sales, and 25 percent of that normally goes delinquent and 10 percent usually gets to the 90-day column, you would have a fairly stable delinquency picture. But if you had a great sales month, and sold $150,000 in that month, your outstanding delinquency would drop drastically in comparison to this larger figure.

You must be able to make such an adjustment to know what your delinquency rate is really doing. Dollar amounts are easy to compare, but percentages are better indicators if they are compared properly. When you do notice improvements or worsening trends, determine why the trend changed.

Rule #5:   Know Your Customer

Obviously, you cannot work with customers effectively if you do not know who they are, what they do, and why they should deal with you. And you need to know more about the customer you regularly contact each month than the one you talk to only every six months. These assumptions should be self-evident. Let's talk about them on a case-by-case basis.

Talk Their Language

It is important that you be able to converse with your customers in a language they understand. Naturally I'm not speaking of English as opposed to Spanish or German, but of the jargon of their particular industry. You don't have to be an engineer to speak to an engineer, but if you plan to ask for payment for the paint he used on his last bridge you should at least know what a bridge is. It is important to know your customer's business if it's a commercial account. Know something about what the company does.

For example, it may be a manufacturer of bicycles. You should know that for a number of reasons. If you can discuss bicycles, you'll automatically establish a smoother working relationship. If you can also discuss trends and inventions in the bicycle industry, you can establish a rapport that can pay big dividends if and when money gets tight and the customer has to decide who and what to pay first. It's harder to say no to a friend.

You should also know something about your own company's value to the customer. Why do they deal with you? Is your service especially good? Is your own product one that they absolutely need in their business, and one that they cannot get anywhere else? This case is rare, but it does happen.

How does your price compare? If you upset or mishandle someone, can they go somewhere else? Those may sound like hard questions, but they're really not—even if the customer has no other source for your product, you are still a professional and should not act with any less respect. But you do need to know such things because, in some cases, you may have to work closely with debtors to help them stay in business so that they can repay you.

In effect, you might be their lifeline. For example, if a debtor is a photographer, and you are the only laboratory in town able to develop pictures from a certain type of camera to certain specifications, you might literally "have the person by the throat." That fact does not excuse your mistreating or hounding anyone for payment; on the contrary, it should mean that you would try especially hard to help the customer manage his or her payments so as to stay afloat.

In dealing with companies large and small, all these guidelines apply. The customer may have dozens of other sources and may need you like the proverbial hole-in-the-head; in that case, knowing the reality, you would do well to maintain an extremely friendly relationship—it might be your one hope. When all other factors are equal in business, friendship carries the day.

You should know how your product is used by your customer. Sometimes you will encounter a customer who is withholding payment because your own company refuses or fails to deliver your product as they require it. Knowing about a customer's business and understanding that customer's position in the marketplace as you do, you can help resolve such a situation.

You might be able to ask your friends in the shipping department to change the shipping schedule for the customer, and they'll do it for you because you've made friends with them, too.

As an exercise to help you understand all your customers, and the interdependence between them and your company, list three reasons why each customer needs your product or service. Try it—the results may surprise you and the benefits may accrue for months to come. You may want to list the information on a customer account card.

Know the Customer's Company Structure

This is a corollary, and again it hardly needs defending. To understand your customer and the relationship between his or her company and yours, you have to know how the company is organized as well as what it does. On the most basic level, you cannot even deal with it until you know who to deal with.

When you send notices to the customer's address, they may never reach the right person until you learn who that person is, and what position he or she occupies in the hierarchy. Here are some basic customer types, with some discussion of their business structure that should help you in dealing with them. Study each one, and decide where each of your accounts fits in the list.

THE INDIVIDUAL—AS A CUSTOMER. If your company is a retail business, you probably deal with individuals as consumers more often than with commercial accounts. There are differences, of course, but basic collection methods still apply in either case.

If you are dealing with an individual, the credit amounts are generally smaller, the products might not be so critical to the customer, and the relationship between you is certainly more direct since you do not have to work through a screen of secretaries and other company functionaries to get to the key person.

But, in either case, be polite and make the same effort with the debtor, win their confidence, overcome their fears and objections, and extract your money. In legal aspects your options are about the same. In general, you may find businesses to be more knowledgeable about the collection laws than the average individual, though this is changing rapidly.

THE ENTREPRENEUR—AN INDIVIDUAL AS A BUSINESS. A business that is owned and operated by one person is known as an entrepreneurship or proprietorship; it differs from an individual consumer in several ways. To begin with, your company's reasons for extending credit to a business are somewhat different than those for which it grants credit to a consumer.

A business owner generally intends to use the credit to purchase items necessary to the business. Businesses expect to make a profit as a result. They can therefore be judged, as a credit risk, both on the basis of what they are currently worth and on the basis of what new revenue, or cuts in operating costs, the new product they are buying will produce.

An individual consumer must be judged solely on the basis of what they are worth, including what their regular, dependable income will add to that value over the time the "loan" is in effect. On that basis, as a consumer, Bill Jones may qualify for a $2,000 credit limit. But as a business he may qualify for a $10,000 or $20,000 credit limit.

Most entrepreneurships are small or medium-sized businesses. They are started and operated by single individuals— who own and control everything.

Many smaller companies operate as a sole proprietorship and this is valid. It is the easiest way to start and it is not as complicated to operate. I will go into detail later about evaluating credit and handling the collection situation for this type of business. But, for now, remember that a sole proprietorship has one person at the controls—you need to deal with that person.

PARTNERSHIPS. Partnerships are very similar in operation to proprietorships in that they are run by individuals who are personally responsible for all the debts of the company. The only difference is that there are more people involved in the ownership of a partnership.

LIMITED PARTNERSHIPS. I have attempted to stay clear of legal matters in this book. I believe the credit industry has relied too heavily on "their rights" under the law in the past and, therefore, have not developed the skills needed to manage the credit/collection function. There is one legal area I would like to touch on at this point, however. This is the role and responsibilities of limited partners.

Interested individuals may invest in a partnership in the same manner as they invest in a corporation. Their role is very similar to that of a stockholder in a corporation. They are not allowed to participate in the management of the partnership, however. An individual may be a stockholder of a corporation and also be an officer of the corporation. Limited partners are not allowed to act as managers of the partnership.

There is always at least one person in a limited partnership that is designated as the "General Partner," and as such is the manager, or managers, of the partnership.

A limited partnership is a legal entity and as such must be filed with local government. When a person that you feel is a partner in a business tells you that they are "just a limited partner" ask them for the document number that was filed with the county government. If they have not filed the document, they are not part of a legal limited partnership, and all participants are general partners.

There is one other difference that few people are aware of and which is very important in credit and collection. While stockholders invest in the company and receive dividends, normally they have no personal liability as far as corporate debts. Limited partners also invest, but their investment remains "at risk" as long as the partnership functions.

The "at risk" concept is what makes limited partners different from corporate stockholders. If an individual invests $10,000 in a limited partnership and receives $5,000 of that back as their share of the profits, that $5,000 is still "at risk" and could be collected by a creditor to cover outstanding debts. This is an important concept to remember if you ever deal with a limited partnership.

If a limited partner has ever received any of his or her investment back, that portion of the original investment is still "at risk" and you might be able to collect a payment of a debt if the partnership is insolvent.

If you are dealing with a limited partnership that has failed, and you are trying to collect your money—look to the limited partners—ask your attorney to check into this possibility.

CORPORATIONS. Corporations are considered "individuals" under the law. They have the rights, privileges, and responsibilities that you and I have. The difference is, of course, that all of the activities are handled by third party "trustees" who act as directors and officers.

Corporations can take many different "guises" or names. They may appear to be an individual, John Smith, Inc., an accountancy corporation; or a partnership, Wilson and Moyer, Inc., a medical corporation. A corporation may also appear to be an association or a cooperative.

While corporations may appear to be different things in different situations, they all should be viewed the same by you. Be sure you deal with an officer or manager who can sign for your product or service. This is especially true in the smaller corporations.

I have been involved in cases where unauthorized people purchased my products and my company was never paid for the products. In court we lost our case because the corporation maintained that our company should have known the office secretary didn't have the authority to purchase an $800 typewriter, even if she did claim to be the office manager. Good point to remember.

One more point before we leave corporations. Be careful in dealing with out-of-state corporations that don't have a good Dun and Bradstreet rating or a good credit listing.

Collecting money from small out-of-state corporations that are solely owned, or owned by less than ten individuals is virtually impossible. Watch out for Delaware and Nevada corporations in particular. Both states only require a street address, which is, for all intents and purposes, a mail drop.

Delaware will also "help" shield the name of the stockholders and officers. Delaware requires the information to be filed but if a person "forgets" to include it, the corporation is still registered and they are sent a letter asking for the information. Try skiptracing that!

INSTITUTIONS AND GOVERNMENT AGENCIES. If you deal with schools, hospitals, or government agencies, you must rethink your approach to credit and collections. Before doing business with this type of customer, a business should sit down and evaluate the risks involved—and there are risks. The main problem is slow pay.

A company that is undercapitalized can easily go under before it has the opportunity to collect the money due it, let alone the late charges.

A large contract, or purchase from this type of customer can be the downfall of a small or middle-size company. There are ways of diminishing this problem, and I go into these in Chapter 4, "Making the Credit Decision." Remember to evaluate the risks before you sell to government agencies or institutions.

Rule #6:   Make It Personal

You should follow this rule as closely as possible. No single statement says it quite as well as this rule. You must conduct business on a personal level. This is the most important point you should learn about your on-the-job conduct.

You must work with a sense of purpose, a sense of personal style, and that should be *your* purpose and *your* style—maintain a personal, one-to-one relationship with your customers that makes it easy for them to pay you and difficult for them to say no.

To accomplish this you must sell yourself first. You already know that, but I want to repeat it anyway. Give the customer a chance to like you. Introduce yourself when you talk to them for the first time.

Find out about the people—or person—you deal with. What do you have in common that you can talk about? Take it a little bit at a time, to ease any tension and maintain a graceful, easy feeling of communication between you. Remember that your work is a continuation of the sale, which is not itself complete until you have completed your job. So learn to use sales tactics in dealing with customers. Take charge. Call the shots. Let them know you're a human being who's interested in them and interested in working with them to help them pay you on time.

Being Businesslike But Pleasant

You must understand that there is a fine line between being a businessperson and being your customer's buddy—but you have to walk that line.

Your real purpose is to help solve the customer's problem in paying you on time. Remember, that to the extent that other conversations and additional information about the customer help you accomplish that, it is all worthwhile.

When you talk to your customers, automatically assume you have the answers for them, and let them know it. Then get to the heart of the problem and help them work it out. At the same time, be warm and personable, but never become emotionally involved.

Always remember that you are working in a business situation. No matter what it may be, do not take it personally. Sometimes your customers will use you as their "whipping boy," if you let them. Sometimes they will tell you troubles you may not believe. Sometimes they will make you want to weep for them—never let them do that to you.

Beware of emotional involvement, and remember what I said about being friendly. Learn to walk that fine line.

You'll hear about more imaginary tragedies than a hundred storytellers could conjure up. You'll be told that you're sending people to the poorhouse, that you're a hard person, that your company is heartless, and a thousand other things. Let it all run off your back, keep the smile in your voice, and ask them once again when they'd like to start paying.

Always Being the Good Guy

You may find it useful to always be the good guy. It is a good game plan to never let the customer identify you personally as the person to whom the money is owed. See that the customer conceives of you as a sympathetic friend, but nevertheless, one who has to ask for the money for the company who insists on being paid for what it has sold.

Establish the fact that something must be paid. Then determine how much and when? Nail it down. Get the customer's commitment just as you would if you were selling the product in the first place. I discuss the actual steps in this process in Chapter 6, "Effective Telephone Collection Techniques."

As an example of always being the good guy, I used to trade accounts with other collectors in certain cases, calling on some of theirs, while they called on some of mine. This was all within the same department, of course, and only occurred when we felt that it was necessary.

We would call the accounts and tell the customer that we were the auditors calling in the place of the regular collector, trying to establish some basic information. Would the customer be paying regularly from now on? Since payment history did not look especially good, why should I believe the customer? You can probably guess what happened many times. The very fact that an outsider was brought into the collection situation helped. I could then refer to the auditor's call—and it worked.

You may feel that we used deceptive practices, but we were actually auditing each other's accounts. We found that, as collectors, we were able to pick up techniques from each other by doing this. I found it very helpful when I first started out. Putting a third party into the collection situation helped the customers renew their commitments.

Knowing the Customer's
Point of View

Through all of the above, you must strive constantly to understand your customer's point of view. You can't really help if you don't know the problem. You can't possibly understand an inability to pay if you don't know that the customer, as a business, is strung out until XYZ Corporation finally makes its quarter-million-dollar semiannual payment. This does happen. Some of your best, most reliable customers may occasionally be strung out by their customers and need extra time to make good on their commitments to you. Understand that. Know about those things.

Never Becoming Condescending or "Better-Than-Thou"

Nothing can kill a good business or personal relationship faster than condescension. Never stoop to it. Never destroy a good thing with such an attitude.

Understand your customers, talk to them on a one-to-one basis, become friendly with them, but do not pander to them or insult their intelligence or their integrity.

In the long run, that tired old Golden Rule still applies in the business world as much as it always has. If you simply treat your customers as you would wish to be treated if you owed money to them, you'll reap the rewards and your company will prosper.

Chapter 3

THE PSYCHOLOGY
OF COLLECTIONS

To BE effective as a collector you must understand the collection situation from the debtor's point of view. You must also understand how the debtor will most likely react to you and your collection effort. This applies whether you work exclusively with commercial accounts or individual consumers.

Once you know who the debtors are and how they are most likely to react to your collection effort, it becomes apparent that dealing with corporations, partnerships, and other commercial accounts is very similar to dealing with individuals in three important areas:

1. They need credit for the same reasons.
2. They abuse credit for the same reasons.

3. They attempt to avoid paying, or evade the collection situation for the same reasons.

In this chapter I'm going to do something no one has ever done. I'll show you why your delinquent customers act the way they do—why some rant and rave, while others try to avoid any contact with you. I am going to go into the heads of your delinquent accounts, and I am going to show you why they act the way they do—and how you can use their own psychological profile to get command of the collection situation.

Profile of the Debtor

The first thing you must know is what causes debtor delinquency. When you understand that in most cases it is a single issue, you will be much better prepared to handle the situation. There are six basic causes of delinquency which I will discuss in-depth.

The True Deadbeat

There is no word in the collector's vocabulary that is more overused and more misused than "deadbeat."

A true deadbeat is generally defined as a person dedicated to getting anything and everything possible for nothing. If this type of person manages to secure credit approval, he or she will use it to the limit, and simply refuse to pay, or stall and make excuses, or disappear. Such an individual will fail to live up to promises with such regularity and in some cases, such outright daring and ingenuity, that you may be driven to distraction if you are not aware of what, and whom, you are dealing with.

Fortunately for all of us the true deadbeat is relatively rare. Because you meet this type of debtor, or someone who seems to be this type, once or twice a week you may consider deadbeats much more common. The truth is that they are the exception and not the rule among debtors.

Once it is established that the debtor is a true deadbeat, who has no intention of paying an obligation, there is only one course of action.

Don't waste time trying to be nice, understanding, patient, and considerate. Bring out the big guns and use all the power you've got. There is no other choice. Use the law to your advantage; start legal action—immediately. Turn the account over to an outside collection agency or lawyer, but don't waste precious time trying to chase this type down once you know what the game is.

The Modified Deadbeat

The modified deadbeat may, at times, behave like a true deadbeat but is really a different animal. The difference lies in the cause of the delinquency. A modified deadbeat is usually someone who had no intention of cheating your company when he or she applied for credit. This type of person may have paid regularly for a long period and be someone with an extensive, and outstanding, credit history.

This type of person becomes what appears to be a deadbeat for any number of reasons: divorce, depression, financial reverses, religious conversion (particularly to one of the cults that requires all property be given to the church), illness in the family; the list of reasons goes on and on.

The important consideration for you is that the modified deadbeat did not set out to beat you out of your payments and may, in time, be reinstated as a regular, paying customer. This is why it is important for you to know something about your customer.

Why does a person who has paid regularly for ten years suddenly fall 30, 60, and 90 days behind? Many times, a good-paying customer suddenly encounters a situation at home or at work that simply cannot be handled. Life becomes out-of-focus and priorities become radically changed. Such a person may find that he or she is faced with a delinquency for the first time in life and simply doesn't know how to handle it. The debtor panics at this new problem and won't face the facts; or other problems may be so overwhelming that this delinquency is a minor priority at this time.

Because the debtor has not faced this type of situation before, he or she doesn't handle it well at all. The debtor will promise you anything just to "make the problem go away" for the time being. While outward actions mimic those of the real deadbeat, inside this person is being torn apart.

The collector assigned to handle this type of customer must decide where to draw the line.

There are no foolproof rules here; knowledge of the customer, knowledge of the company's rules, and some basic understanding of human nature must be used to arrive at a decision as to how far you should go in trying to work with a modified deadbeat. Patience, consideration, and understanding may be rewarded in kind, or you may lose the battle and wind up with egg on your face. If you know your customers and do not become emotionally involved, you'll find that most of your decisions will be correct in the long run.

"More Important" Things to Do

Occasionally you'll run across a debtor who simply has "more important things to do" than paying bills. He or she may be a person with plenty of money, who is in all other respects a pillar of the community, but who simply will not take the time to deal with creditors in an orderly, businesslike fashion. In such cases, you have to step in and lay down the ground rules. You may have to call on a certain day every month, send reminders regularly even when the customer is up-to-date, and in other ways simply "shepherd" the customer through an orderly payment cycle. When the customer has the money but is simply too busy conducting personal affairs, such as traveling around the world, you may need reams of patience in dealing with him or her, but at least you know you will get paid eventually. As a collector of some ingenuity, it is up to you to determine how and when.

The Overextended Debtor

Overextended debtors are the real casualties in the credit crunch. They're the credit cripples created by the last few decades of easy credit, available to everyone. Over extended debtors come from all walks of life, from all the social strata. They may be wealthy businesspeople who simply do not know when to stop buying new cars and new clothes; they may be poor cleaning people who simply do not realize that every item charged to that department store account will, one day, have to be paid for.

In dealing with overextended creditors, your best bet is to work out payment plans with them based on their real income and their genuine ability to pay. Don't let them con you as easily as they con themselves into believing they can handle more than is realistic. They've already proven they're in over their heads; make them see that and force them, if necessary, to deal with their indebtedness in realistic terms.

In many cases this will mean a cutoff of further credit until their account is brought current; sometimes this will amount to a permanent termination of credit privileges and an unfortunate blot on their record. Do not feel, however, that you are being forced into making such arbitrary, potentially devastating decisions for these people; obviously they are making them for themselves by failing to handle the basic financial responsibilities entrusted to them in the first place.

In general, your attitude toward overextended creditors should include kindness and consideration but should, above all, include firmness and fairness for both of you.

Major Catastrophe

Occasionally one of your customers will encounter a major catastrophe in his or her personal or business life that will radically alter the ability or inclination to pay. Medical emergencies, automobile accidents, natural disasters like floods and landslides, robberies, criminal proceedings—all these eventualities can take a normal credit situation and completely turn it around in one day. When such things happen, you have to make some basic decisions on behalf of your company, usually with your manager's support and approval.

When a man's wife suddenly contracts cancer and requires all his money for treatments, do you press him to the limit for payment of a $300 note? When his child dies in an automobile accident and he loses two months work from distress, do you push him to the wall to collect the $80 car payment that month?

Those are relatively easy cases from your standpoint; believe me, they get harder. Think of yourself as a social worker in some instances; you have to work with people, understand their problems, and help create solutions for them just as you would if you were a social worker assigned to their case. The only difference is that, as a professional collector, your ultimate loyalty must be to your company and you must endeavor to look out for the company's interests as much as possible.

Your guidelines should always be to be friendly, understanding, kind, gentle, and patient. But—do not get emotionally involved. Always promote business decisions based on a human approach to these very real problems.

One special case is the collector in the medical profession, who is attempting to collect the amount of a bill not covered by insurance, or the entire amount from a person with no insurance. In most cases, you are collecting money billed for an emergency procedure, and therefore completely unexpected in the patient's budget. You must work very closely with this type of account to be sure *something* is paid each month.

Lost Income

Debtors will sometimes get behind in their payments because

they lose income for one reason or another. Something in the "major catastrophe" category could be the cause; something else relatively minor could also be at fault. Perhaps John Jones' company laid him off work for two months because a truckers' strike in Minnesota halted shipments that his company needed to stay active. Perhaps he was required in court for two weeks and was not paid for his time.

Whatever the reason, when one of your customers loses a significant amount of income, you will want to work with him or her to assure a smooth flow in payments to you, and to avoid saddling the customer (and yourself) with a needless delinquency record.

The Collection Situation as a Modified Sales Situation

To help you understand the collection situation, let us look first at the traditional sales situation.

Why do people buy? What forces propel them to a buying decision that favors one item over another, one company over another, or one payment plan over another? In answering any of those questions we could write another entire book, but let us examine at least some of the answers in simplified form.

Why People Buy

People usually buy for one of the following reasons.

They need to be fulfilled. Many believe that a particular product will "do" something for them in a very real sense: make them more attractive, more desirable, more intelligent, or more qualified to do any number of things.

The product itself. People are often sold on the value of a particular product through advertising, the product's reputation among their friends, or their own personal experiences with it. In short, they believe in it and they believe they need it.

The source of the product. Many believe in the company or the person who produces the product. They believe it has to be good since it comes from so-and-so. They attach a value-by-association to it that may or may not be genuine but which is, nevertheless, real enough to them.

The value. The product itself has an intrinsic value or is inherently valuable to them by virtue of a service or a feeling it alone can provide. Maybe it's a three-hundred-year-old postage stamp that has both high market value among collectors and a high personal value to the buyer, who derives a feeling of pleasure and pride from ownership that equals the cost of the stamp.

The time to buy. Some people simply have the money and the time to spend it. It's as easy as that for them. Or, in other cases, a particular item at home or at the office has worn out or served its usefulness, and it's time to buy a new one. The boss says, "Get downtown and buy us a new coffeepot; this one's had it!" and the employee scurries to the car, petty cash in hand, to do his bidding. For that person "Now is the time to buy."

The Selling Situation

When a prospect approaches a product, what sequence of events normally ensues? In a typical situation, the salesperson tries to establish contact and inquiries discreetly (if he or she knows how) about the prospective customer's intentions. Is the customer just looking? Would he or she like to see a particular type or model? Would the prospect be interested in this brand-new upgraded model over here, the one with the yellow paint job and the air-conditioned add-on unit?

The salesperson attempts to do two things at first: try to determine the prospect's buying "attitude" and try to stimulate interest in his or her own version of the product the prospect had in mind. If the prospect wants to buy a coffeepot, the salesperson tries to convince him or her, without hitting the person over the head with logic, that this coffeepot is the best on the market for the money.

All this is part of the sales presentation, which a good salesperson launches into as easily as a skin diver breathes under water. (With a little practice it becomes second nature.) The sales presentation can be as simple as holding up a set of matching towels, or as complicated as demonstrating the functions of a computer in a sequence of operations that requires two weeks to complete.

In all of this, the salesperson attempts to create *a desire to own* on the part of the prospect. This is accomplished by trying to make someone want something badly enough to pay for it—it's as simple as that.

How a salesperson does this may depend on a number of factors: the product, the customer's need for the product, the time of day, the need for a demonstration, or the facilities at hand.

Eventually the salesperson comes to the "close," in which he or she must either complete the sale or lose it. Good salespeople show their colors here; bad ones, conversely, generally lose the sale at this point. The close involves asking those painful questions and getting the names signed on the contract, and some people simply cannot seem to do this.

Even as all this occurs, in the mind of the would-be buyer certain considerations are crowded rather closely together. Is the salesperson making invalid claims? Will the product actually do what it's supposed to do once the customer gets it home? Will that performance be good enough?

What about the price? Is it too high? Is the customer losing money by failing to "shop around" a bit longer? Does Acme Company across town have the same thing for 10 percent less? Is it worth the trouble to drive over there and find out?

And what about peer disapproval? Will Bill Jones next door make smart remarks about the new car? Will tough-as-nails Al Jenkins, his father-in-law, laugh at the new washing machine and tell him what he should have bought? Will the members of her bridge club approve of her new carpeting? Will the other kids think this baseball glove looks too cheap to be any good? Some of these questions may seem silly but they are real questions and they pop up in the minds of buyers. Everybody fights with the same doubts, fears, and concerns.

On the other hand, what about the benefits the customer can derive from buying such-and-such a product? Will it really make her more attractive? Will it really improve his work output, or make his secretary more efficient? Will the new lipstick really look good on her, or will the new tires really make her car easier to handle and better on gas? Some of these may sound like objections but they are not; they are considerations of the benefits customers expect to derive from various products. You can add to this list forever, until you have a book of your own.

The salesperson learns to balance benefits against objections; ideally pointing out two benefits every time the customer comes up with one objection. Or the salesperson may find some other way to demolish an objection, perhaps by a simple application of logic. Many objections are not real anyway, but are simple ploys used by customers to avoid making a buying decision, or to feel they're fully justified in making the one they want to make.

The Collection Situation

The collector's objectives are like the salesperson's. For the short term they want to inspire a fairly immediate payment on the account. For the long term, they want to inspire regular, consistent payments on that same account until it is paid to date or paid in full. In the similar manner, the salesperson wants to make a sale right now, but he or she also wants John Jones, the customer, to come back next week and buy something else.

To accomplish these objectives, collectors must understand the product and its real benefits to their customers. A talk with one of the sales force could help with this task. They must also know their customers, as we have already pointed out in-depth.

There are the benefits of the product that can be stressed to delinquent customers, but there are also benefits to up-to-date accounts. For one thing, they won't have the collector calling so much. Also, they'll sleep better at night. In fact, they may still have a place to sleep, since the company won't be taking the bed back if the debtor makes the payment. Or their house. It should be easy to identify benefits for the customers—there are many good, legitimate reasons out there waiting to be pointed out.

To find out some of the best reasons, talk to someone (the top performer) in sales. As a practice exercise the collector might even want to list the most common reasons, then keep the list at hand, ready for use whenever he or she runs into a reluctant payer. Include the most basic, obvious reasons (peace of mind, freedom from fear) and some of the more extreme reasons (repossession, continued distress).

As a collector works with the customer, all the usual objections are heard; you must learn to overcome these naturally by pointing out some of the benefits. Eventually, though, you will come to the real objection. There is always that one real reason (in our listing of delinquency cases we identified six of the most common reasons).

Most objections will involve one or more of those basic reasons. But you cannot do anything to help the debtor until you have identified that real reason, so dig for it and do not give up or be satisfied until you know you've found it. Then you can go to work on a solution that works out best for everyone involved.

In the collection situation, the "close" comes when you and your customer agree on a payment schedule that satisfies both of you. In other words, the customer can meet it and you, as a company, can accept it. This new schedule may closely resemble the original schedule, or it may involve much smaller payments spread out over a much longer period of time. You, your company, and the customer make those determinations together; remember, nothing has truly been accomplished until you reach this stage.

The Debtor's Frame of Reference

All debtors that the collector deals with have their own frames of reference from which they see themselves, your company, and the collection situation they now find themselves in. Let's consider some of the elements that make up that frame of reference.

Your Company's Image

First of all, the debtor has a particular image of your company. This may be an entirely accurate image formed by experience and an uncommon capacity for seeing things as they really are. However, most debtor frames of reference are colored by subtle considerations the debtors themselves may not even be aware of.

For example, they may recall past buying experiences with your company that may or may not have been entirely pleasant. If they were hassled by a salesperson, or mistreated by a clerk, or overcharged at the cash register, they may harbor some very strong resentments. If they were treated with utmost courtesy by the salesperson and by everyone else who had contact with them, they may have nothing but goodwill for your company.

At the same time, their own objective experience with the product also colors their attitude toward the company. If they had an unhappy experience, they will blame the company. If they had an unusually good experience, they may feel very positively toward the company. If experiences over the years have been both good and bad, feelings toward the company may be correspondingly ambivalent.

Also, the real importance of the product to them tempers their attitude toward the company that sold it to them. Do they wish they had never bought it? Has it been a problem for them? Has it ever worked? Has it always worked? Did it help earn the money they expected? Did it slow business down? Did it save a life? Did it cause an accident? All of these questions should be answered—any one of them might identify a very important consideration for the collector that is stepping into the situation.

Finally, debtors probably have some recall of previous collection effort, by your company or by someone else's company. Even if a collection effort has never been directed toward some persons, they may know someone who was hassled or heard stories about collection techniques. Before collectors say a word, the debtors automatically paint them with a certain brush in their mind. The collectors need to know that in the very beginning, because they must deal with it directly if they intend to work out a good solution with the customers.

Customer's Recall of Past Experience

The customer's own recall of past collection experiences strongly influences the frame of reference. The customer interprets any action the collector may take, and any overtures the collector may make, in the light of what has happened before. In this respect the debtor reacts in accordance with the experiences in one or more of several categories. Let's examine some of these.

SUCCESS VS. FAILURE. Psychologists tell us that people arrange all experiences into two groups: successes and failures. This is a common human tendency; we all do it. It is part of the natural inclination to protect the self (or ego) at all costs. Thus, we tend to remember successes and we try to forget failures, or we change the facts and subtly alter the details to reflect more favorably on ourselves. If the debtor has had "successful" dealing with previous collectors—that is, dealings that were resolved without damage to his or her own self-image or standing in the community—the debtor is more receptive to collection attempts because of the hope to repeat the same "success" experience.

However, if previous experience is considered a mild "failure"—that is, in any way at all unpleasant, either in a personal or business sense—the debtor automatically, subconsciously anticipates another "failure" in dealing with the collector and reacts accordingly. He or she certainly doesn't look forward to talking to the collector or attempting to work out a solution.

INTENSITY AND PROXIMITY. The intensity of a previous experience, and the customer's proximity (or nearness) to it both directly affect outlook. If there was a powerful, dramatic, and thus "intense" experience with a previous collector, the debtor subconsciously reacts toward the current collection situation in a more intense manner. If there was a very low-key, mild experience—neither particularly good nor particularly bad—the debtor tends to regard the current collection situation in the same noncommittal way, expecting nothing at all in particular to come of the experience.

Proximity works much the same way—if the experiences were more recent, they are fresher in the debtor's mind and the reaction is more directly influenced by them. If, for example, there was a very, very unpleasant experience with another collector just two weeks before, this memory is especially fresh and the taste lingers, so the debtor will be correspondingly unreceptive to the current overtures. On the other hand, if there was a good experience recently, the debtor may welcome this call and consider this a chance to settle things and ease his or her mind.

Knowing about these factors ahead of time can help the collector tremendously in knowing what to expect from the customer. Of course there is no way a collector can know about a call from another company—but if your company uses different collectors for the same account, a good record of what took place last time should be available in the customer's file.

FREQUENCY. Frequency of experiences is another consideration to be applied as directly as intensity and proximity. If the customer has had frequent experiences with collectors, those experiences tend to color a reaction to the current collection call far more than infrequent experiences do. The more an experience is repeated the more it becomes reinforced in the memory, for good or bad. And fortunately or unfortunately as the case may be, most experiences are remembered in either of those two lights . . . good or bad.

REMEMBERING THE PAST AS THE PRESENT. Salespeople encounter customers who remember "the way things used to be" all the time. A customer will say, "Boy, if they just made widgets like they used to!" Or, "How can you charge me $50 for this when I paid only $20 just ten years ago?" The world changes every day; debtors sometimes choose to remember facts from the past that tend to cast them in a better light. "I had a better job two years ago; keeping up with payments was much easier then." "I can't believe the way the interest rates have gone up in the last three years; you guys are killing me with interest rates and service charges!" The collector hears all these "excuses." They all reflect the unconscious inclination on the part of debtors to remember their old payment at the lower interest rate. And consistently they bring these facts up to the collector almost as though he or she were responsible for the changes in the world that make living more expensive and more complicated for the debtor.

ILLUSION. Sometimes customers object strenuously to the dollar amount they owe your company. They may claim it is too high, that they could not possibly have bought that much, or that the items were not worth the price. They may be stalling or simply arguing with you to avoid payment, or they may actually be reacting according to their own illusions about the situation.

In such cases, illusion works this way. Suppose a customer bought an expensive woodworking machine from your company. The machine itself cost $4750. When purchased, the salesperson also sold the customer a $600 set of woodworking tools, $300 worth of imported woods for use in making fine furniture, and a years supply of finishing materials, expecting to buy more only as he or she needed them.

But by comparison with the cost of the basic machine, those accessories just didn't seem that much more expensive at the time of the sale.

What is $150 compared to $4750? The customer bought the accessories under the self-induced "illusion" that they weren't very expensive, that since they had already paid nearly $5000 for the machine he or she might as well fork over another few hundred and get the other items needed.

Now, many months later when the account is delinquent and you call to attempt to bring it up-to-date, the accessories suddenly seem very expensive as do the woods and the finishing materials. The customer is not sure he or she wasn't cheated; talk of suing for price gouging among other things, follows.

If you should encounter a customer that is talking like this, probe to find a possible reason for the customer's thinking and be prepared to deal with it by putting things in perspective. Remember, putting things in perspective goes both ways. Check out the sales department and find out if your company has a sales "policy" of running up the tab, or if certain salespeople tend to do this.

Trying to make the sale as large as possible is the nature of selling because salespeople are most often paid on commission. Therefore, they are more in control of their earnings than other workers. To get the highest pay, you sell the most you can. It is far easier to sell an add-on to someone after the "buy decision," than it is to get the next prospect to the buy point.

Go ask the sales department to help you understand what is happening here. It is another way of building bridges and learning how things are done in your company.

ORDER AND COMPLETENESS. Throughout all of this discussion, I've been touching on a behavior principle that simply stated is: People like things to be orderly, complete, and balanced. They tend to reject images that are not good. You can probably see it at work in many of the previous illustrations.

It is important for you to be able to apply this principle. People tend to remember things that reflect favorably on themselves, in business and personal situations. They forget things that do not reflect favorably on themselves. They also tend to change things, and change the manner in which they recall things, to allow themselves to feel "smart," or "superior to the situation," or "competent in all things."

In dealing with customers in the collection situation, most people recall events, in a manner that protects themselves and reinforces their own notions of themselves and the world around them. And take those considerations into account when you ask for the money.

The Customer's Self-Image

The collector must also deal directly with the customer's self-image since this, too, influences the reaction to the collector, as a person, and the collection situation. In general, most people's self-image can be separated into two distinct halves: the "me" each person thinks he or she is versus the "me" each person wishes he or she was.

Most psychologists agree that when those two images merge in a person's mind, that person achieves inner peace; conversely, the conflict so evident in most personalities is usually associated with the disparity between those two poles of the self-image. You don't need to be a practicing psychiatrist to recognize some of these basic conflicts in the people you meet in a collection situation.

Sometimes they will try to be "big, strong, and bold" with you because they are afraid to be that way with other people. They may assume a far more offensive, aggressive pose than is normal for them because you represent a threat to their own private world in which all forces try to equalize themselves and promote peace of mind. Their reactions to you may also take totally different forms, ranging from outright aggression to downright submission, and only experience can teach you to recognize the causes and deal with the real problem instead of the symptoms.

It is important for the collector to understand the customer as much as possible. Only when the collector has some awareness of all the forces at work can he or she truly work with the customer in the best possible way.

Working hand-in-hand with some of the self-image factors, certain status needs also contribute to the customer's need for the product, his or her need to satisfy or elevate self-image, and therefore the reaction to you when you ask for payment for the merchandise.

Status Needs

Other conditioners are also linked directly to the debtor's self-image, and therefore influence his or her reaction to you and his or her performance in the delinquency situation.

For example, in certain ethnic groups it is part of the cultural heritage to be free from debt. Therefore, people from such backgrounds will always do everything in their power to avoid delinquency on any bills. When they do get behind, the delinquency is a source of great embarrassment and genuine concern for them. Knowing this in advance, you can avoid making the experience any more unpleasant than necessary for them, especially since you know you're working with people who really want to pay.

In the same way, some people are taught certain habits in regard to bill paying and financial responsibility that reflect more on the quality of the person's upbringing than on any intention to defraud, avoid payment, or act irresponsibly in any way. People do develop habits in paying their bills—they may get used to paying all bills on the fifteenth of the month, or they may habitually allow their secretary to do it for them. Any change in amounts owed, due dates, or other aspects of their obligations may not "compute" in their system and may not be handled properly until new habits are formed by such debtors.

Personal ethics and morals (they are much the same thing) come into play in a number of ways. The true deadbeat, for example, obviously subscribes to a personal ethical system that allows stealing from companies like yours with no moral compunction whatsoever. The modified deadbeat may suffer pinpricks of conscience when he or she first gets behind, but after a period of months he or she may get so used to being delinquent that it no longer affects such a person's conscience, and may eventually lead to feeling no sense of responsibility toward a creditor at all.

People who get behind as a consequence of a great catastrophe, or a period of lost income, may suffer inwardly—they may feel shame, embarrassment, mortification, anger—any number of emotions because of their inability to pay.

Also, because of built-in prejudices against bill collectors, promoted by stories most debtors have heard sometime in their lives about unscrupulous collectors and underhanded collection techniques, many debtors will not only automatically resent any attempt by you to effect collection but will openly fight you in what they see as an act of "principle."

They are victims to their own prejudices, fueled by hearsay evidence to the effect that all bill collectors are reprehensible, uncaring, unfeeling parasites who prey on the good guys in society. And naturally enough, every debtor considers himself or herself a good guy. You are the bad guy, even though he or she is the one who bought the Cadillac with no hope of ever paying for it on time.

How Does the Debtor Defend Himself—and Why?

By now we have established a number of reasons for debtor delinquency. We have looked at causes, we have examined the collection situation and compared it to the sales situation, we have discussed the debtor's frame-of-reference and self-image, and we have identified a number of factors that help develop that frame of reference and that self-image. Now—what does the typical debtor do when he or she gets behind? What specific behavior patterns will you, as the collector, have to deal with? Let us look at some of them.

Everybody in modern society comes equipped with certain built-in defense mechanisms—or so it seems. Debtors, especially delinquent debtors, usually have more than their share, perhaps because they especially need them to survive.

Typically, when you first contact delinquent debtors, they will make one or two basic attempts to save face. Very often they will insist on reconstructing the situation for your benefit, filling in all the details, hoping perhaps to convince you that they are not really at fault; that it's someone else's fault that they have not paid on time. The delivery man brought the new pool three days late, so they shouldn't have to pay for it. Or the salesman told them they wouldn't have to make a payment on the new car for three months, and for heaven's sakes—they've only had it four months now!

You'll constantly be amazed at the ingenuity displayed by debtors in trying to absolve themselves from blame while passing it on to someone else. (Think what wonderful politicians most career debtors would make.) Nothing is ever their fault—they may be sitting with three gallons of ice cream and 300 pounds of prime rib stored in their new freezer, but they'll be damned if they'll pay for the freezer, by god, because three flakes of paint came off the first week.

Debtors will perform basic surgery on the truth in three simple ways: They'll deny the facts, they'll change them for their own benefit, or they'll totally disguise them. If you know they bought a new stove on the fifteenth of the month, they'll say they never did. If you say they're four months behind, they'll explain that the machine didn't work for one month; therefore they're only one month behind (huh?). Or, if you ask them why they haven't made a payment for three months they'll suddenly become very vague and before long they'll be "somebody else" and the person you thought you were talking to is "not home now."

All these techniques give the debtor time to construct a new self-image or erect a new facade. Something must be done to save an ego and salve a conscience, assuming one still exists. So ways are found to deal with indebtness that do not personally denigrate the debtor in any way. He or she becomes the good guy in his or her own mind, and can therefore hide behind a new story or a brilliant facade that covers up the truth and allows the debtor to believe he or she is "not guilty." That's why debtors can suddenly become such good liars when they've been honest men or women all their previous lives.

In all of this, the debtors usually have recourse to one of five or six basic courses of action. We've already talked about some of them in general terms—now let's get specific and identify them for you.

First of all, the debtors may ATTACK. They may instantly assume an offensive position and try to put you on the defensive. This may be done by attacking your company or its product. In some cases they will attack you personally. Other times they will attack society in general, the government, their in-laws, and anything else that gets in the way in an attempt to shift the blame, divert your attention, and direct the thrust of your collection effort into some other direction.

Or they may try to EVADE you. They may do this by answering you vaguely, without admitting anything or giving you any useful answers or information, or they may do it by avoiding your calls and your requests altogether. They are never home. They are never in the office. If you do catch them by surprise, they're on the way to an important meeting, but don't worry—they'll call you back in the morning. Such mornings never come!

They also may try to RETREAT or SUBMIT. If they retreat, they'll backpedal so fast you'll have trouble catching up on that score alone, and when you do you'll be told, "O.K.—take it back. I don't want it." Obviously, that's no solution since the newly purchased car is no longer new and is not worth what the buyer was supposed to pay for it. If they submit, they'll agree to do anything, very pliably, trying to get you "off their back" so they can forget about you until you call again.

Sometimes submission is genuine—in other words, the debtors realize they owe your company, recognize their obligation to pay, and submit to your suggestions for repayment whether they include a large immediate sum or a more manageable payment schedule. This may lead to a legitimate AGREEMENT between you that will systematically resolve the indebtness and clear up the entire situation. That kind of agreement is always what you're working for.

Why do the debtors indulge in such shenanigans in the first place? Hundreds of reasons can be given, but we'll limit ourselves here to some of the basic examples—many of them you already know. But why do debtors behave so "crazily?"

We have already talked about some of the answers. We don't need to go through them all again here. If you remember that all debtors try to do one or two basic things, you'll remember enough to deal with most situations.

They always strive to *protect and preserve their self-image.* They try to *save face.* They react to you in ways that sometimes change their own self-image for better or for worse—hopefully, if you can cause them to react to your collection effort in a mature, responsible manner, you can help them to improve their own self-image by helping them do the proper thing.

Remember that most of their reactions satisfy some need or desire that may be lurking below the surface in their personality. Perhaps they need a chance to be aggressive toward someone. You may be just a convenient target. Perhaps they need a chance to preserve their status in the community and maintain their self-image, which you can give them by working out a reasonable payment plan that does not embarrass or unduly inconvenience them.

Remember too that you are dealing with a "buying" attitude on the part of the debtors, in the sense that they will reject or accept you—there is not much middle ground. If they absolutely reject you, avoid you, lie to you, curse you, you have little choice in dealing with them. You cannot very well work out an agreement with someone who will not talk to you, so you'll have to use the impersonal techniques (letters, telegrams) and eventually end up sending them out to collection.

If they accept you, at least partially because you're a caring, intelligent human being who understands their situation and does not embarrass, revile, or persecute them, they will probably work out a solution with your help that will be best for everyone concerned. Only then does your company save money and improve its cash flow—by effecting collections in an orderly, proper manner that brings in the money, on time or nearly on time, in a smooth, predictable flow.

And there, in a nutshell, are the twin objectives of all collection efforts—to solve the problems now, in the short term, and thereby assure a smooth flow of payments and a consistent reduction in delinquency in the long term. That's what it's all about. Meet the problems head-on now, before they develop into bigger problems, and thereby assure a smoother future both for the debtor and for your company—and FOR YOU.

Chapter 4

MAKING THE CREDIT DECISION

T HE CREDIT policy of your company should be consistent in all respects with the overall company goals, objectives, and policies.

Customers should be given a written statement disclosing all credit terms and other conditions required of them to receive credit from your company.

In this chapter I discuss the procedures that you should have in place for the credit checking/granting aspects of the credit/collection process. These are the first steps that must be taken on every credit decision.

During the credit checking and credit granting process your department should perform the following tasks:

1. Gather information.
2. Evaluate the information.
3. Accept or reject the credit application.
4. Establish credit limits, if applicable.
5. Communicate your decision to the applicant, and any departments within your company that need to know your decision.

These tasks should be completed in a timely, but orderly manner, using all credit sources that are applicable to the individual application in question. There is a fine line between quick turnaround and thorough investigation. You must get the credit decision as quickly as possible, but you must get as much relevant information as possible to make a good decision.

The Purpose of a Credit Evaluation

There are two reasons for gathering and evaluating credit information.

1. To determine if the applicant *can* pay the account within your company's terms
2. To determine if the applicant *will* pay the account within your company's terms

Gathering Information

You must use a standard format for collecting credit information. Most companies give a credit application form to the applicant to fill in relevant credit data.

There are three types of credit accounts for which you may be responsible. You may deal with all three, or a combination.

The Consumer

Consumers are individuals who request credit to buy personal items. These are nonbusiness related products. You need to get the full name and address of all the persons relevant to a credit application. There are many cases where two or more people might be listed on the credit application.

- Primary creditor requires a cosigner.
- Husband and wife may be automatic cosigners. If you don't know the laws of your state, ask your legal department or company attorney about your specific requirements.
- Coresidents may be applying for credit. People living together may not be married, but may have long-term commitments to each other.

Commercial

Commercial accounts are businesses buying your product for use in their business. There are three categories of normal business accounts.

Proprietors are business owners who have solely owned businesses. In most cases you want to get both the business credit information and the personal credit information. The exception might be for a large solely owned business.

Partnerships require at least the name and address of all *general* partners. We cover the nature of partnerships in Chapter 2, "The Rules for Success." You do not need to know the names and addresses of any *limited* partners at this time.

There are special partnerships where you do not need to get the names of all general partners. These are large law, accountancy, and medical partnerships. The partners are all general partners and are all responsible for the debts of the firm, but they have delegated the management of the business aspects of the partnership to a managing general partner. In most cases the credit information from the firm is all that is required.

Remember, general partners are responsible for any debt incurred by any of the other general partners.

Corporations come in two basic types. These are:

1. Closely held corporations
2. Public corporations

The *closely held corporation* is very much like the normal partnership or proprietorship. It is a business that is owned and operated by a small group of people, normally no more than ten shareholders.

The *public corporation* is one that has stock that is openly sold on the public market. This type of corporation is tightly controlled by federal, and in many cases, state law. There is far more validity in this type of corporation saying that personal credit information is not given by officers and directors.

However, if you have a public corporation that has a bad credit history, or no credit history, you can reasonably ask for personal guarantees from officers and/or directors of the corporation. After all, you are granting a privilege to the buyer.

When you require a personal guarantee from an officer or director of a corporation, have that person sign the contract twice. The first signature should include the person's title, and the second signature should say, "as an individual."

This second signature leaves no doubt as to the status of the signator. He or she cannot come back at you if the account goes delinquent and say that he or she was merely acting as an officer or director of the corporation and has assumed no personal responsibility for the debt.

Key Accounts

A *Key Account* is a commercial account that docs not require the normal credit gathering and investigation. Credit applicants that fall into this category are:

1. Major corporations (Fortune 1000)
2. Schools
3. Hospitals
4. Government agencies

If you ask a major corporation or any type of government agency to fill out a credit application, they will not give it to you. But the information that you must have for this type of account can be labeled as key account profile information. You can get the information you need, and the customer does not feel you are asking for too much information. I discuss this special category of customer later in this chapter.

I have not called this category of credit applicant "key account profile" because it will always be one of your high volume accounts. I have selected this name because you or your sales representative will have to get the information from the applicant. If your sales representative produces a form titled "Credit Application," the person requesting credit terms will probably balk at giving the data. But if the sales representative produces a form entitled "Key Account Profile," the reaction will be just the opposite. This form is used to play on the applicant's ego. See, you *are* part of the sales team.

Required Information

The specific type of information that you get is dictated by the type of customers your company has. If you grant credit to consumers, you need information that is not relevant for business customers. If you grant credit to businesses, you have specific requirements that don't carry over to the consumer market.

The Name and Address

You must get the correct name and address for all applicants. If more than one person is signing the contract, get all names and all addresses.

If the applicant is a subsidary of another company, get the parent company's name and address. Likewise for a government subagency.

Social Security Number
(Consumer Only)

The social security number is required from an individual applying for credit, and from any company official who may be personally guaranteeing a company debt.

This is used to establish the positive identification of the applicant. In many cases the applicant's name is common enough that there are two or more people in the general area that have the same name. The social security number is used to positively link your applicant with his or her credit history file.

Type of Business

You should require the business applicant to indicate the type of business structure. Many of your credit decisions are made based on the structure of the business.

Bank References

You want to get all of the bank accounts that the applicant has. This is to the applicant's interest during the credit evaluation, and to your interest if the account goes bad.

Trade References

The applicant should be able to give you two or three current creditors. Be sure to get the account number; everybody uses them today. Consumers may give you gasoline credit cards, but gasoline companies don't rate their accounts. These accounts are worthless to you.

Local business references are essential for commercial applicants. If you seem to be the first company granting credit to a company—BE CAREFUL!

Likewise for consumers. If the applicant is over 21 years old, it is hard to believe that they have been on an "always paid cash" basis. Be careful to verify residence in this case. The person may have just moved to town, leaving a horrible credit history behind.

Close Relative (Individual Only)

The requirement for a close relative is for later use. If the account is delinquent, and turns out to be missing, you can then call this person to find out where the customer is.

If the applicant appears to be suspicious, you may want to verify the close relative. Call and ask if this information is true. I would also verify that the close relative exists by looking in the phone book. It is easy to have a friend assume the identity of the close relative. If the prospective customer is trying to "scam" you, they will probably have this prearranged, and you will not be able to confirm this close relative—but be on the lookout.

Employment and Income Information (Individuals)

Normally, you want the current employer and a salary range. Most companies only confirm that the person works there, and that they are within the salary range you give.

If the applicant wants the personnel department to give more information, it is his or her responsibility to get personnel to give it to you. This generally requires a written request by the employee. You can always ask to see a pay stub.

If you have insufficient information, call the sales department, or whoever is waiting for the approval, and say that you need more information from the applicant's employer.

Financial Statements

This type of financial information is generally restricted to commercial accounts. But you may be in a situation where you are selling to a consumer and want a personal financial statement.

There are two grades of financial statement. The first is *audited* and the second is *unaudited.*

An audited financial statement is prepared by a certified public accountant, and all entries are verified for accuracy. These financial statements are very expensive and are not generally prepared for small companies. Public corporations are the primary source for audited financial statements.

An unaudited financial statement is only as good as the person who has prepared it. Some companies prepare their own financial statements. Any computer system that is worth having can be used to prepare a good-looking balance sheet and income statement. Many of the better ones prepare statements of change for areas such as working capital or inventory.

In the past, creditors have been able to request financial statements and rely on their relative accuracy. But, in the world of the "PC" (personal computer), it is simple to create financial statements that make the company look as solid as a rock.

Financial statements simply are not as good a financial evaluation tool as they used to be. Even if they are prepared by a certified public accountant, they are only as good as the CPA's judgment, if they are unaudited.

Information From Your Investigation

Your credit investigation should not take more than 48 hours. If you see that you are going to take longer, let the proper person know. You should also give an indication as to when you will complete the check. This may happen when the person is from out of town, or the application requires some special type of clarification.

Confirmation of All Information Listed on Credit Application

Your credit check tasks are broken down into two groups. The first is to verify information that is related to credit payment history. This means name, address, occupational information, bank accounts, and other similar data.

You must attempt to confirm as much of this information as possible. Call the reference, identify yourself and your company. Then ask if the information on the application is true.

Trade/Credit Payment History

The second part of the credit research is to gather information about the applicant's credit payment history. This is information at the credit bureau, as well as information that you may be able to validate directly with the applicant's creditor.

Lawsuits, Judgments, and Other Pertinent Legal Information

The credit bureau should have all of the legal information about the applicant in its files. The records show all legal actions such as lawsuits, judgments, garnishments, bankruptcies, and divorces.

You must know how your local credit bureau works, and what information it stores, and most of all, how you get it and how much it costs.

Current Financial Condition

If you deal with commercial businesses, you need to assess the current financial condition of the business. As I said, this is difficult because financial statements are so easy to generate using financial programs on small computers.

If the financial statements have been prepared by a CPA, your chances of getting valid information are much better than if the applicant has generated his or her own.

A word about CPAs. As with any profession, there are good CPAs and poor CPAs—there are conservative ones and liberal ones. Some are willing to stretch a point to help their clients. They may evaluate the worth of property on the high side. The validity of the information you receive is only as good as the person who prepared it.

In general, if you have an applicant who provides you with financial statements that have been prepared by a CPA firm, you can have a high level of faith in their validity.

Special Credit Checking Procedures

When is a credit check not a credit check? Right, when you check large corporations, institutions, and government agencies. Let's face facts. You are not going to get any government agency to complete a credit application.

But when a major corporation or government agency wants to do business with your company, the credit check is not one of checking past payment history. It is an attempt to determine the company's paying procedures.

These types of customers do not require a normal credit check, in most cases. But beware of assuming financial stability simply because of high visibility. Check with your local commercial credit agency, or Dun and Bradstreet, if you have any doubts about the company.

Because a corporation is large and profitable, and because government agencies have exemption from credit evaluation, doesn't mean that they pay on time. In fact, you will discover (if you don't know it by now) that these accounts are the slowest payers.

This section outlines some of the procedures you can take to resolve the problems with big business and the government; at least where your accounts receivable are concerned.

Large Corporations and Government Agencies

There are steps that you can take that give you a good start toward getting this type of account to pay within your company's normal payment terms.

Figure 3 shows a key account profile that has worked wonders for me wherever I have used it.

NAME AND BILLING ADDRESS. Name and billing address are two very important pieces of information. They account for a great many delays in payment. The company accounting department cannot pay for something if it has not received an invoice. You need to put the entire name exactly as it must appear on the invoice. If the customer is a division or subsidiary, the name of the parent company should be shown. If this is a subagency of another government agency, this relationship should be filled in on the form.

TELEPHONE NUMBER OF ACCOUNTS PAYABLE. This telephone is important also. There are cases where subagencies and subsidiaries have the parent as the accounts payable entity. You should know this if it is true for a customer.

KEY CONTACT. The key contact is the person that you can contact if trouble arises. If this account is going to do a large volume of business with your firm, get a contact name—even if it isn't from the accounts payable office.

PURCHASE ORDER CYCLE REQUIREMENTS. The requirements are different with all cases, so get the following information at acceptance, or even as a condition of acceptance:

Figure 3. Key account profile.

Key Account Profile

Organization : _____

Billing Address : _____

Attention : _____

Key Contact : _____

Telephone No.: _____

Are Purchase Orders Required Before Delivery? ☐ Yes ☐ No

   ☐ Verbal Number Okay

   ☐ Must Have Physical P.O. in House

Can An Order be Shipped on a Requistition Number Only? ☐ Yes ☐ No

   ☐ Verbal Number Okay

   ☐ Must Have Physical P.O. in House

Typical P.O. Number : _____

Significant Numbers : _____

Are Blanket P.O. Numbers Issued? ☐ Yes ☐ No

Schools, School Districts, Hospitals and Organizations that require Board approval

Normal Monthly Board Meeting _____

Send Invoices by : _____

Attention: _____

A *typical purchase order (PO) number,* and the meaning of the numbers, if it is important.

The *most significant digits/characters* on the PO. If you work with the federal government, you know that agencies can issue a series of PO numbers, and that only the last few numbers have any significance.

Remember the story I told in Chapter 2 about the government account that always paid slowly because the PO number was being cut off. This is the way to get around this type of problem. When you deal with the government this information is important. Get it from the customer.

Blanket PO numbers are common for companies that do business with service companies. The company issues a PO with a "not to exceed" amount. If you have this type of customer, you should keep track of your billing amounts, and when you see the end coming, call it to the attention of the sales department and have it get a new PO.

Can a *purchase requisition* be accepted as a firm order? This is very important. Some companies give their management a great deal of freedom, while others require an approved PO before an order can be placed. If you have a company that has given you a purchase requisition as an instrument for a firm order, be sure it is valid. Most likely you will get paid in the end, but if you go around the purchasing department of many companies, they resent it and will put off the approval for payment.

Schools and Hospitals

When you work with schools (individual schools or school districts) and hospitals, you must get all of the information above, plus some very important additional information. The most important is the day of the month for the monthly board meeting. In some cases schools and hospitals require board approval of all invoices before payment. In most cases this is simply a "rubber stamp," but if you miss the board meeting by one day, you have to wait until next month to be paid. It is sad but true. Find out if the schools and hospitals you deal with have this requirement. If so, know the board meeting date each month.

Note: If your company does business with an organization that has a board that must approve all payments, be sure to send the invoices well before the meeting date. Since this should be one of your special handling accounts, you should have a key contact at the organization. Make an agreement that you will mail ALL invoices, in one envelope, to your key contact a week before the board meeting. This will make payment a smooth, regular operation.

Sources of Credit History

Performing a credit check can be different, depending on your location. In different parts of the country, business is conducted in individual and unique ways, and the credit function is no exception.

Principles of Credit Gathering

Wherever you live, and whatever mores your business community adheres to, there are some general principles that you should abide by.

RECIPROCITY. If you normally call other companies for credit information, you must remember that you will also be called. If direct checking is used in your area, give the companies that call you the same attention that you want to be given. The way you respond will soon be known by the credit community, and if you are rude and slack when you give information, you will soon be treated that way when you need information.

CONFIDENTIALITY. All credit information is confidential. If you talk about it outside your company, you could be placing yourself and your company open for a lawsuit.

When I was a credit manager for General Electric Credit Corporation, the credit bureau gave me a confidential item about one of the applicants I was investigating. The item was that the applicant I was investigating was a known narcotics (hard stuff) user. This information would normally make the decision very easy.

But my problem was that I had to reject the application, without being able to tell my customer (an appliance dealer), why I couldn't accept the order. He would not accept the generalization of bad credit history; he wanted to know the items, and I could not tell him. It sounded to him as if I didn't want to do business with him any longer. It caused a problem for a short time, but I lived through it. The information you deal with is given to you for one reason, to permit you to make a valid credit decision. Guard the information as if it were your own.

VERIFICATION. One of the major tasks in credit gathering is validation of the information. You must have a procedure in place that will validate as much of the information on the credit application as possible. This means the name, address, telephone number, employment, and credit history.

Individuals. The best method for checking the name is through a state driver's license, company badge with the individual's picture, or some identification that has both the name and a picture of the applicant.

Never use a social security card; you have no way of verifying the validity of the card.

The fastest way of verifying the address is through the telephone book. The telephone number can be verified at the same time. There has been a rule in the credit community that a person must have a telephone to qualify for credit terms. This is an excellent rule to follow.

Employment is verified by calling the employer. Be careful to verify the name and address of the employer through the telephone book. If you do not find the employer in the telephone book, ask the applicant to verify the existence of their employer.

Local Businesses. You can verify the information given by local businesses through your local business exchange, or check directly with the creditors listed on the application. You can also use the Dun and Bradstreet Reference Book; have Dun and Bradstreet do a complete credit report. The D & B Credit Report is similar to the one you get from the local commercial credit exchange.

Major Corporations. There are thousands of national and international companies that may wish to do business with your company. Some of the names you will recognize immediately, while others will be completely unknown to you.

If you subscribe to the Dun and Bradstreet Reference Book, you should use it as your first point of reference. If the company is in the book, and if its rating is good, you can use this to accept the credit. However, this only means that the company exists, and it has an overall financial stability. When you have this type of situation, you must get the Major Account Profile Sheet completed.

Government agencies are sometimes very difficult to validate. When I was an instructor at IBM, one of my students told me about having a government security agency as a customer where it was impossible to do any type of validation, so they had to take the government purchase order as the validation.

When you first do business with a government agency, it may not be possible to verify its validity except for the purchase order. Require a hard copy of the PO before you ship your goods. When you get the PO, attempt to contact the purchasing department to validate the name and invoicing address. When you contact purchasing, complete a Major Account Profile Sheet over the telephone.

Hospitals and schools are easy to verify. If you can't find a hospital or school listed in the telephone book, find out why. It will probably be because it is brand new.

THE AGE OF THE INFORMATION. When you receive information from the credit bureau look carefully at the "last updated" date. If the date is more than a year old, have the credit bureau do an update. The age of credit information is extremely important. A person can go from excellent to bankrupt in a six-month period. If the credit history is over a year old, you must get newer information.

Direct Sources of Information

There are two methods of getting credit history information. You can call the creditors directly, or you can use the local credit bureau to gather the information.

ADVANTAGES. The advantage of doing a direct check is the personal contact that you have with the other creditor. You may be able to find out things about the applicant that a credit bureau would not get for you. You should establish a set of questions that you can ask during your direct checking. You want to know if the person rating the account also collects delinquent accounts. If so, do they know this person or company. If they know the account, is it from working with the customer. In most cases the person who is rating the account will not give you any information beyond the normal credit history, but it is worth trying.

DISADVANTAGES. The disadvantage of direct checking is that it is very time consuming. Because you have to invest your time in direct checking, it is far more costly than a credit bureau report.

If you rely entirely on a direct check, you are not assured of getting a complete picture of the applicant's credit history. Most people who fill out credit applications only list their good creditors. If they have a bad account, it will most likely not be on the credit application.

If you use a credit bureau, you can make one call and get the entire credit history. You must weigh the advantages of talking directly to the other creditors, against the time you must use to get the information.

Beware: Some states prohibit direct credit checking. Find out about your state laws.

Indirect Sources of Information

There are three basic sources for getting consolidated credit information. These areas are shown below.

LOCAL CREDIT BUREAU. The local credit bureau most likely handles only individuals. In some cases small towns have a single credit bureau that handles all credit inquiries. You need to know how this is handled in your location.

NATIONAL ASSOCIATION OF CREDIT MANAGEMENT. The National Association of Credit Management has affiliate offices throughout the United States. For the most part, you can rely on the information that you get from one of these offices. Find out if your commercial credit exchange is an affiliate. If it isn't, it would be wise to check out its validity. One thing that you should do if you deal in commercial credit is to join the local credit managers association. Check around and I'm sure that you will find that there is an organization that meets once a month for a luncheon meeting. It will be well worth the time to attend.

DUN AND BRADSTREET. Dun and Bradstreet has been in the credit reporting and evaluation business for many years. In most cases the information you receive from it is good. You should try to meet with the local D & B staff if possible because the information you get is only as good as the people making the evaluation. I have found that the level of expertise seems to vary greatly across the country.

OTHERS. I taught a seminar for Advanced Credit and Collection Techniques for IBM for a couple of years. During this time I tried to get a picture of the credit evaluation services that the IBM offices used across the country. I found that it varied greatly, and that the credit management personnel in each office had to evaluate the options open to them.

I found that the National Association of Credit Management affiliate offices were the most consistent. You should check out the sources available to you.

Evaluating Credit Information

The amount of time that you spend checking credit information must be related to the amount of credit being requested. In some cases your credit items will be so small that it isn't even worth spending any time clearing credit.

One example I can think of for this type of situation is the local newspaper. The home delivery fee is not the major source of revenue for this business. Advertising is the main source of revenue, and copies delivered establishes the advertising rate. The monthly fee for delivery is very small in comparison to the revenue received from ads.

Now you may say, "But the delivery is generally collected by a young paper carrier," and you are correct. But I am thinking about newspapers that bill the customers directly. This is one example of a situation where no "up front" checking is done. There are very few of these types of businesses.

You should consider the following information when you make your credit evaluation.

Length of Time in Business/Buying on Credit

The time that a person has been using credit, or that a company has been in business, is important. Stability is the key here. Older, more established individuals or companies, who have used their credit wisely and paid their bills on a timely basis, should be considered for a higher credit line.

As with all rules there are exceptions. Physicians are generally considered good credit risks. New doctors or dentists can be considered for a higher than normal credit line based on their profession.

Some businesses have the same kinds of special credit line rules. A company may be a brand new start-up, but if it is a wholly owned subsidiary of a nationally known and respected corporation, you can generally go by the parent company's credit standing.

Last Date File Was Updated

The age of the credit information is important. If you find that a credit file at the credit bureau is more than a year old, have it updated. It is easy for an individual or company to go from excellent credit status to marginal in less than a year.

If you do have a file updated, get a copy of the old file and the updated file. This gives you an opportunity to do something that you cannot normally do. Using the two credit payment profiles, you can get a comparison of the payments. This comparison can show a company, or individual, that is starting to slip in their payment pattern.

The trend of payment can indicate whether an applicant is credit worthy. You may see a small trend and decide that the applicant is still credit worthy, with a lower credit limit. If you find this type of customer, flag the account and monitor the payments for a few months.

Type of Business or Employment

The type of business for a commercial account, and the employment of a consumer, are closely related when considering an applicant for credit.

COMMERCIAL. The type of business is very important when you deal with commercial accounts. You should consider the following points:

- Trends of the company's industry sector
  —Glamour industry, solid mainline, or old declining.
  —Industry on an upswing, downswing, or very stable.

—Is it a new industry? We are seeing a number of infant industries growing up around us. You should know what this industry is and what chance the applicant company has in making a go of it.

- The position of the applicant in the industry
  —A new company entering a highly competitive industry.
  —A mainstream company well established in its industry.

- A mainstream company or a unique company
  —What makes the company unique? Is this good or bad from the credit point-of-view?

There are many questions that need to be answered. These are just a sample of the types of questions you should be asking.

CONSUMER. The type of employment is a strong consideration in granting credit. You should consider the following items:

- Where does the applicant work? Is it a large solid company, or a small company that might not be in business next week? Is this company one that tends to keep its employees, or are there regular layoffs? Is the company in an industry that is seasonal, such as construction?
- What is the applicant's position? Is it the presidency, or an entry-level position? Or, is it in the middle somewhere? Business executives are considered one of the soundest credit risks. The reason is that they have an image to present to both the outside world and their corporation.

Income

Income is always an important consideration. Whether you deal with consumers or commercial accounts, you must determine that the applicant has sufficient income to pay on the debt.

COMMERCIAL. There are many reasons for getting as good a determination on income as possible, but I would like you to consider one area that is not talked about too often. How will your company's product or service influence the applicant's income?

If your company markets a product that influences your customers' income potential, you should consider what effect it is going to have. An example is an advertising agency. The agency is in business to enhance the client's income. If the present income level is too low to qualify for credit, and your company has made claims of being able to raise this level, it is only fair that you include this new income level when you evaluate the applicant's credit worthiness.

CONSUMER. It is important to consider the amount of income that a person makes on a monthly basis. Finding the applicant's income level verifies one of the two main questions asked in granting credit, "Does the applicant have sufficient income to pay the debt?"

Current Obligations

The current obligations that an applicant has directly affects the chances for repayment on a timely basis.

The following information is given by consumer credit bureaus and commercial credit clearing organizations:

- Type of company, generally indicated by a Standard Industry Code (SIC) code. This is a standard industry rating established by the federal government.
- Date account opened.
- Date of last purchase.
- High credit limit.

- Terms (2–10, N–30, 12 × $18)
  The 2–10 means 2 percent discount if paid in 10
  days. N–30 means net, invoiced amount, if paid in
  30 days, and the 12 × $18 means 12 monthly pay-
  ments of $18.
- Amount now owing.
- Amount past due, if any.
- Payment history.
- Comments about the account.

In addition to this information, consider the following
for each type of applicant.

COMMERCIAL. The current credit obligations should be
considered in the same way as income. If your company's
product is going to increase the customer's cash flow, you
should take this into consideration.

CONSUMER. Current obligations include:

- Rent or mortgage payment.
- Utilities.
- Credit obligations.
- Other situations that influence the amount of dis-
  posable cash the applicant has each month. For ex-
  ample, an individual may appear to have a great deal
  of disposable cash until you consider things such as:
  —Alimony payments
  —Insurance payments made for children in high
    school or college
  —Car payments for children in high school or college
  —Special medical programs that are not covered by
    insurance

Payment History

The applicant's payment history gives you the answer to
the second question in the credit analysis process, "Will the

customer pay the account within terms?" This answer is deduced from the person's, or company's, payment history.

All payments do not carry the same weight when you are evaluating credit information. The way a person or business pays their rent does not necessarily reflect the way they are going to pay your company. Consider the following:

> *The importance of the item.* Not all items that are purchased have the same value to the buyer. Rent or mortgage and a car are probably at the top of the list. From there down it is really a matter of the individual's priorities. You should consider how the accounts have been paid, and where your product is going to fit into the applicant's priority list.

> *Previous credit limits.* You must compare the high credit the applicant has been given in the past to what you are going to give. You do not want to make great jumps in credit limits. A person or business must slowly build the right to credit by showing responsibility.

> *Payment history.* It is important to consider who the applicant has been paying in the past. If there are slow pay accounts, who are they, and are they similar in nature to your company.

>   If a commercial applicant is on a COD basis with a company, you should know what kind of company it is. Some companies do not grant credit, but require COD. If an applicant shows COD from a company, and you have questions about it, ask the credit bureau to check it out, or call directly yourself.

Bank References

The bank accounts listed on the credit application show the type of bank accounts and the current balance. You should attempt to get all bank information if possible.

The credit bureau will list bank information in the file. See if the credit application and the credit file agree. If the credit bureau lists accounts that are not on your application, have the file updated, or check all accounts directly.

Normally you will get:

- Date opened
- Average balance
- How the account has been maintained (bounced checks)

Your Product's Effect on Monthly Obligations

I have mentioned this in a couple of the sections, but I think this is a very important area, if you deal with commercial accounts.

Many companies sell products that help their customers increase revenue or cut expenses. If your company's products are in this category, you need to carefully consider the product's impact on the applicant when you are making your credit decision.

You may not even think of your company's product having anything to do with expendable cash, but if you think about what the products really do for the buyer, you may find that the product can create enough cash flow for a marginal account to receive credit.

If your company has never looked at its products in this light, do an analysis and if you find that there is a case to be made for this point of view, tell the sales department. Show it you are on its side.

This chapter presents a brief analysis of the areas that you should consider in your credit analysis. For a more in-depth analysis of the credit checking process see Chapter 7, "Credit Granting Procedures."

Chapter 5

ESTABLISHING A WELL-STRUCTURED COLLECTION PROGRAM

An EFFECTIVE and dynamic collection program is not simply a money retrieval system. It must be an integral part of the total sales process. The main objective of the collection program must be to develop customer relations and recover the company's delinquent receivables as quickly and economically as possible, while encouraging the formerly delinquent customer to patronize the company with future good business—business that is paid within the credit terms.

The Criteria for an Effective Program

An effective collection program has three main qualities:

1. A clearly defined strategic program for each type of account
2. A well-ordered progression that is timely and time effective
3. A clearly understood central message that pervades the entire program

Clearly Defined Strategic Programs

There are three strategic programs that are used to collect delinquent accounts receivable.

1. *The paper program*—This strategy permits a program to be highly effective and cost efficient.
2. *The telephone program*—This strategy is the focal point of any effective program.
3. *Customer visits*—The most effective strategy available for an entire class of misunderstood customers.

A well-structured collection program uses all three of these collection strategies. Each strategy is most effective for a specific type of delinquent account. It all comes down to dollars invested versus dollars outstanding. This means you use the least expensive, the paper program, to collect the low-dollar accounts, and the higher cost methods to collect the high balance, or high-volume accounts.

If your collection program is to be the most effective you can design, you must take the time to analyze your receivables file, and determine how each type of account is going to be handled. I will show you a process that you can use to analyze your accounts receivable file to determine the appropriate action for each of your accounts.

Your collection efforts must be time effective since your personal time is limited. You must invest it in those activities that will return the best dollars per hour. After all, time is one of your finite resources. If you spend the same amount of time attempting to collect your $10 accounts as you do collecting your $10,000 accounts, you are wasting a valuable resource.

A Well-Ordered Progression

To make your personal efforts time efficient, your collection program must also be timely. Your delinquent notices must go out on time, your letter program must be timely, and your collection calls must be made on a regular schedule.

Each step of your collection program must be in a logical sequence, because each step builds on the previous ones. It would be very foolhardy to simply go through your accounts once a month and send everyone with a 90-day delinquency a COD letter.

It is important to follow an organized program that progressively leads up to the final COD letter where necessary, while allowing the delinquent customer to respond in a positive manner. You must always give your customers a chance to tell you the reason for their nonpayment.

The Central Message

Your collection program must be consistent and it must carry the same message throughout. This message should say, "Hello, our records indicate that your account is past due. If there is a problem with the billing, or if you cannot pay the total amount at this time, please contact (a real person's name) at (telephone number) and we will work together to come to a solution. If there is no problem, please pay the outstanding amount by return mail. Thank you."

This is a short, generic message that you can use as the basis for your first notice. It condenses your central message, and the tone of your entire collection program.

Until you have a firm reason to believe that a customer is not playing straight with you, always treat the customer as if you know he or she is going to respond to everything you say in a positive manner. It's the self-fulfilling prophecy in action. It gets results.

You should use the following guidelines in all your collection activities:

Be personal and friendly—Remember without most of these folks, your company would not be in business. Most of your delinquent customers are not chronically delinquent.

Motivate them to action—Your collection program is in place to get the delinquent customers to bring their delinquent accounts current as quickly as possible. Each part of your program must motivate them to do this.

Offer a way to save face—This is especially true in the telephone calls and the personal visits. Approach your customers in the same manner that you would approach a person whose friendship you value. Allow them to offer a solution. Attempt to find the real problem, and propose a solution that gives them a way out.

This is particularly important in situations where your company has allowed a delinquency to go on over an extended period of time. By the time someone decides to take action, the customer may be in over his or her head. Make the customer a part of the solution. Work together to come to a plan that is fair for both of you.

Fortify a positive self-image—You must always feed the positive self-image of your customers. Some of them don't have much positive self-image left, but if you hold out a hand and offer fortification to their souls, they will react in kind. It might sound corny, but it works.

Appeal to Their Status Needs—Oh yes! Stroke 'em. As I say in Chapter 3, there are all types of people, and many, many reasons why they are delinquent. But they all have certain common needs. And pushing the right button will bring in the jackpot. It is the way successful salespeople have performed for years. Remember—you are a sales representative—use your sales tools.

The Paper Program

The paper program is the framework for all your collection activity. It is very simple, and it must be carried out on a regular, timely basis. Consistency is the key word.

It starts as the first reminder notice that most of your customers receive, and it ends when the attorney/agency letter is sent telling the customer that the account has been assigned to an attorney or collection agency for final action.

It may be used as an alternative to telephone collection calls or personal visits for a small segment of your accounts, but it should be integrated into your telephone program to augment its effectiveness.

The paper program becomes very important in the badly delinquent cases. If you have to place a customer on COD status, you must notify him or her of your action. If you make an agreement for a payment plan with a customer, either by telephone or in a personal visit, you must follow up immediately with written confirmation of the agreement.

If you plan to turn a customer over to an outside collection service, you must notify the customer of the pending action and give him or her a chance to take a positive step that will stop your action.

And finally, the paper program is used to reinstate a customer who has taken appropriate action to bring the account back into order.

The Components of the Program

The paper program is made up of the following series of notices and letters that are sent to your customers on a predetermined schedule.

STATEMENT/FIRST NOTICE. The exact form that your first notice takes is determined by the nature and the size of your company.

Companies That Send Statements. If your company sends a statement to each customer at the end of each month, you can easily insert, attach, or stamp your first collection notice at this time. This may be done by hand in small companies, or generated by a computer for companies that have their notice program on a computer system.

Companies That Do Not Send Statements. If your company does not send statements, your first past due notice is going to be a stand-alone document. This first notice can vary in form from a simple card reminder to a formal letter.

The First Notice Message. The first message you send should be a close representation of the generic message that I mentioned in the beginning of this chapter. Let's take a close look at that message.

Hello, our records indicate that your account is past due. If there is a problem, please contact (a real person's name) at (telephone number) and we will work together to come to a solution. If there is no problem, please pay the outstanding amount by return mail. Thank you.

1. Begin your message by saying "Our records indicate. . . ." This is a soft opening. You have given your company an out if there is some type of mistake in the billing. Never start by saying things like, "Your account is now past due," or "You have failed to make this month's payment." This type of opening leaves you backed into a corner if your company has made a mistake in either the billing or in applying the customer's payment.

2. Never make a direct indictment to the customer on this first contact. The last part of the opening sentence says, "that your account is past due." You are placing the focus on the account and not on the customer. If you were to say something like, "you are past due," you would not only be grammatically incorrect, but you would be openly attacking the customer. Remember this is a *first notice,* not the final COD letter.

3. Next, openly face the fact that there may be a problem. You have not said what type of problem, so you have left an opening for a problem caused by your company, or one that the customer might have in paying the account current.

4. The last part of the notice asks the customer to contact someone at your company. Give the name and telephone number of the person to call. This is far more personal than simply giving a telephone number, or worse yet, just asking for a call. A name is very useful here if it is appropriate in your situation.

SECOND NOTICE. The second notice is the only part of the collection program that I feel is optional. In many cases a second past due notice is too costly to administer. The only time that I would send a second past due notice is if the accounts receivable collection program is computerized, and the computer has been programmed to automatically print out the past due notices.

It is a matter of cost again. If the past due notice program has to be handled by a human being, it is too expensive to have. I strongly suggest that you go directly to the first collection letter (see Figures 4 and 5), or place the account on your telephone collection list, depending on the dollars outstanding.

The message of the second notice is much the same as the first. I would add a couple of sentences that say . . .

> Your account is now twenty days past due. If there is a problem with our billing, or if you cannot pay the account current at this time, please contact . . . so that we can resolve this problem before it becomes worse.

This points out the lateness and opens the problem area a little more. The customer may be more prone to respond with these two additional prods.

The first collection letter is sent to customers that you do not plan to contact by telephone, or that you plan to call in the later part of the month. Customers that receive the first collection letter have low dollar balances and generally fall within the accounts that you have decided not to contact personally.

You may not wish to use the past due notice program, and you may want to start your collection activity with the first collection letter. This is especially true of the small business that does not have a computerized collection program.

As Figures 4 and 5 show, the first collection letter can take a number of forms. The exact form you use will depend on your program and the place that the letter fills.

Note. The second collection letter and the COD letter are used by companies that have "open accounts," and their customers regularly buy the product, or receive service. For companies that have financed their product over a period of time and don't have open accounts, go directly from the first collection letter to the "attorney/agency letter."

THE SECOND COLLECTION LETTER. The second collection letter is the first strong statement that you make to

Figure 4. First collection letter (without statement).

Owen International, Ltd._____

44 City Parkway South
Suite 2200
Anaheim, California 92808
(509) 238 - 9000

Dear Customer,

Enclosed is a statement of your current account status.
Our records indicate that some of these items shown are past due.
We would like to clear up those items and would appreciate a few
moments of your time to help do so.

Would you kindly fill out the bottom portion of this letter and
return it to me in the enclosed envelope?

Thank you for your attention to this matter,

Sincerely,

Frank Lee Speeking
Credit Manager

Please check the appropriate box(es)

☐ Payment will be made by

☐ Please send a copy of invoice #

☐ Please send a copy of work order for the above invoice(s)

☐ Paid on Check # _____ dated _____ deposited _____

☐ Other: _____

_____

_____

_____

_____

_____

_____

_____

Figure 5. First collection letter (with statement).

Owen International, Ltd._____

44 City Parkway South
Suite 2200
Anaheim, California 92808
(509) 238 - 9000

                                                        August 14, 1988
Nemian and Sons
4671 Katella Drive
Orange, California 92666

Dear Customer,

The following invoices appear on our accounts receivable file as
past due. We would like to clear these items and would appreciate
a few moments of your time to help us do this.

Invoice	Date	Amount
AB1555	04/30/88	56.98
AD5630	05/13/88	672.00
AR8851	07/04/88	98.73

Would you kindly fill out the bottom portion of this letter and return it
to me in the enclosed envelope?

Thank you for your attention to this matter,

Sincerely,

Frank Lee Speeking
Credit Manager

Please check the appropriate box(es)

☐ Payment will be made by _____

☐ Please send a copy of invoice # _____

☐ Please send a copy of work order for the above invoice(s)

☐ Paid on check # _____ dated _____ deposited _____

☐ Other: _____

         _____

         _____

the past due account. An example of the second collection
letter is shown in Figure 6.

   The letter states that you have contacted them recently,
asking if there is a problem with their account. Because
they have not responded, you assume that the billing is

Figure 6. Second collection letter.

Owen   International, Ltd._____

44 City Parkway South
Suite 2200
Anaheim, California 92808
(509) 238 - 9000

August 17, 1988

Mr. John Johnson
Johnson Construction
2467 Anaheim Blvd.
Suite 100
Orange, California

Dear Mr. Johnson,

This is to inform you that your account has become seriously
delinquent.

According to the terms agreed upon, ". . . delinquent accounts
are subject to suspension until brought current." We must now
request that payment be sent without further delay.

If your remittance is received in full by August 30, 1988, we will
maintain your account on an open basis. Otherwise, make notation
that all future orders must be paid C.O.D. until the balance is paid.

Of course, if you feel that any of the charges to your account
need explanation, please do not hesitate to call me.

Sincerely,

Frank Lee Speeking
Credit Manager

accurate. The final statement is that if you have not received
payment by the date stipulated, their account will be placed
on a COD basis, and you will be forced to take additional
collection action.

THE COD LETTER. Figure 7 shows an example of a COD letter. This letter is sent to the low dollar accounts that do not respond to collection letters. It is also sent to customers that you have contacted by telephone or a personal visit that have not followed the agreed upon payment plan.

The letter states the total amount due, that the customer's account is now on a COD status, and that if the customer does not respond to this letter, the account will be turned over for final action within ten days.

THE ATTORNEY/AGENCY LETTER. Figure 8 shows an example of an attorney/agency letter. This letter is written so that it can be used for either an attorney or a collection agency. The letter informs the customer that the account has been placed with an attorney or agency, and that all future correspondence should be directed to that office, not yours.

THE REINSTATEMENT LETTER. The reinstatement letter is used to notify the customer that the COD status has been lifted and the account has been given "open account" status. You should always restate the credit limit if your company has set limits. This letter is very similar to the original credit approval letter.

The Timing of the Program

The month is the basic time unit of measurement in collections. At the end of every month you should add up your delinquency and determine how well you have done your job.

Your collection program should be managed in increments of two weeks. There are two dates that should trigger the activity of your paper program; these are the first of the month and the sixteenth of the month. You should be sending notices and letters every two weeks. If there is any magical secret in the collection field, it is the disciplined timing of the collection program.

Figure 7. COD letter.

Owen International, Ltd._____

44 City Parkway South
Suite 2200
Anaheim, California 92808
(509) 238 - 9000

November 14, 1988

Duck and Weave Inc.
1200 Superior Tower
Irvine, California

Gentlemen,

This is to inform you that because your account is
delinquent and no attempt has been made on your part
to bring the account current, we must place your purchase
terms on a COD basis.

You have not replied to notices sent to you regarding
your account.

In the absence of word from you, we assume there is no
question concerning your account. Since it is now long
past due, we insist that payment be sent without further
delay.

If payment is not received in full within 10 days, we
will be forced to assign your account to our (attorney or
agency) for further collection action.

Sincerely,

Frank Lee Speeking
Credit Manager

On the first and the sixteenth of each month you should
examine your entire delinquent file and determine how old
each account is and what action should be taken. The
following action should be taken on the first and the six-

Figure 8. Attorney/agency letter.

Owen International, Ltd.

44 City Parkway South
Suite 2200
Anaheim, California 92808
 (509) 238 - 9000

November 30, 1988

Duck and Weave Inc.
1200 Superior Tower
Irvine, California

Gentlemen,

This is to inform you that because we have not received a
reply to our letter of November 14, 1988, your account
has been placed with our collection attroney for legal
action.

In the absence of word from you, we assume there is no
question concerning your account.

Since this account is now being handled by our attorney, all
further correspondence should be directed to the office of
Hanlman Fast, Attorney-at-Law, 8947 East Street, Costa Mesa,
California 92689. The office may be reached by telephone at
(714) 555-0988

Sincerely,

Frank Lee Speeking
Credit Manager

teenth of the month for every account that you have predetermined to be on the paper program.

10 days beyond normal terms: Accounts whose oldest item
is 10 days past terms should be sent a first notice.

16 to 29 days beyond terms: If you are using a computerized notice program, send the second notice at this point.

30 to 45 days beyond terms: An account that is 30 days or more past due should receive a first collection letter if it has not received a telephone call, or is not scheduled for one in the next 15 days. This is the point where an account is handled by the most appropriate method, depending on the outstanding dollar amount. I show you how to determine this breakpoint later in this chapter.

46 to 60 days beyond terms: This is the time for the second collection letter if the account is being handled by the paper program.

61 to 75 days beyond terms: It is now time for the COD letter.

76 to 90 days beyond terms: If you have received no response by this time, and the account balance is below the telephone program breakpoint, send the attorney/agency letter. You should use the 15-day period here to give the customer adequate time to respond to your COD letter. The letter may say 5 days, but with the time it takes you to put together the letters and the mail time you can use the extra few days.

The Telephone Program

The telephone collection program is the center of your collection program. The personal contact that you make with this collection tool can make you a force for positive action in your company.

There are two types of accounts that fall into the telephone collection category. These are:

1. Special handling accounts—There are four types:
   - Accounts that your company management has said are not to receive collection notices
   - Large corporations
   - Institutions such as hospitals or schools
   - Government agencies
2. Accounts with delinquent amounts that meet your telephone account criteria

Special Handling Accounts

Your company probably has certain accounts that management sees as key accounts. These accounts do not receive past due notices or letters, and they may even be handled by a member of management.

If you do have accounts that have been classified as key accounts, or special handling accounts, they should go at the top of your list for review at the beginning of the new month. If these accounts do not receive notices, it is especially important that you know their delinquency status.

The other class of account that should always receive a call is the large, high-volume account. In most cases it is not useful to send these accounts any past due correspondence. Large corporations, institutions, and government agencies are part of this classification. This group requires special handling, so I am dedicating a section later in this chapter to the special procedures and techniques you use with them.

So your first step is to make your list of special handling accounts that require a call this month.

Coordination With Paper Program

To be effective in your collection activity you must determine which accounts are going to receive your personal attention and which accounts will be handled by notices and letters.

In this section I will explain the method that you can use to make this determination.

DEFINING WHICH ACCOUNTS GET CALLS. To determine the appropriate collection method for each delinquent account, you need to have an aged accounts receivable delinquency listing that is spread by "current," "30-day," "60-day," and "90-day and older." Figure 9 shows a sample Aged Accounts Receivable Delinquency Listing.

Note: If you do not have this type of listing, you should ask your management to get a computer program that keeps all open invoices in a computer file, and lists them by age as shown in the example.

In the last section in this chapter I explain how computers can best be used in the collection program and the types of computer programs you should have.

When you determine which accounts are to be part of your telephone program, you rank them using two factors. The first is the age of the oldest item in the account. The second measurement is dollar value. This permits you to be the most effective and gets the highest return on your labor.

You add names to your call list for the month based on oldest and largest dollars. If you are just starting with this program, you may find it a bit difficult to determine the priority between oldest and largest. If you have never looked at your accounts receivable file in this way before, use the following procedure to rank your accounts:

1. *Run an adding machine tape of the 90-day column.*
2. *Rank the accounts on the tape by dollar value.* I would guess that you will find that a small number of accounts makes up the majority of the 90-day dollar delinquency. I have found that the 80/20 rule works in most cases that I have investigated. This means that 20 percent of your 90-day accounts make up 80 percent of the 90-day delinquent dollars.

Figure 9. Aged accounts receivable listing.

OWEN INTERNATIONAL   ACCOUNTS RECEIVEABLE DELINQUENCY LISTING   PAGE 37
                          PERIOD ENDING: SEPTEMBER, 30 1988

4529	GREEN & BARSTOW, INC	JANE BARSTOW	(714) 555-0921			
INVOICE	DATE	CURRENT	30-DAY	60-DAY	90-DAY+	TOTAL
S56742	05/23/88				94.30	94.30
S62137	06/08/88				103.55	103.55
S78083	07/26/88			56.33		56.33
TOTAL				56.33	197.85	254.18

4654	HASKINS AUTOMOTIVE	ROBBIN SMITH	(213) 555-6840	***** SPECIAL PAYMENT PLAN PER H. OWEN ****		
INVOICE	DATE	CURRENT	30-DAY	60-DAY	90-DAY+	TOTAL
S21219	02/03/88				678.00	678.00
S21219	03/15/88				-100.00	-100.00
S21219	05/02/88				-100.00	-100.00
S21219	06/23/88				-100.00	-100.00
S21219	08/26/88				-100.00	-100.00
TOTAL					278.00	278.00

SPECIAL

4872	HORDCARE PHARMACY	JOHN HORDCARE	(714) 555-5533			
INVOICE	DATE	CURRENT	30-DAY	60-DAY	90-DAY+	TOTAL
P45222	04/13/88				23.86	23.86
P45223	04/13/88				43.75	43.75
S78990	07/29/88			56.85		56.85
P79985	07/29/88			156.96		156.96
P79986	07/29/88			237.80		237.80
S89416	08/24/88		73.75			73.75
S97601	09/26/88	60.00				60.00
TOTAL		60.00	73.75	451.61	67.61	652.97

5013	IMAGES, INC	KYLE BROWN	(818) 555 4700 EXT 336			
INVOICE	DATE	CURRENT	30-DAY	60-DAY	90-DAY+	TOTAL
S53510	06/15/88				83.95	83.95
S53510	06/30/88				-75.00	-75.00
S68956	07/29/88			75.00		75.00
P71564	08/05/88		43.78			43.78
S85193	09/19/88	75.00				75.00
TOTAL		75.00	43.78	75.00	8.95	202.73

5236	JONES HARDWARE	AMY HATHER	(213) 555-1200 EXT 12	*** ATTORNEY ACCOUNT ***		
INVOICE	DATE	CURRENT	30-DAY	60-DAY	90-DAY+	TOTAL
S23490	02/09/88				95.75	95.75
S25616	02/11/99				87.50	87.50
S29745	02/16/88				150.60	150.60
P32161	03/14/88				58.90	58.90
TOTAL					392.75	392.75

SPECIAL

5549	KIELY & SONS	AMBER LOUIS	(818) 555-9800 EXT 43			
INVOICE	DATE	CURRENT	30-DAY	60-DAY	90-DAY+	TOTAL
P58901	05/31/88				180.96	180.96
P58901	06/10/88				-100.00	-100.00
P58901	07/14/88				-50.00	-50.00
S76292	07/18/88			23.65		23.65
P98342	09/30/88	34.55				34.55
TOTAL		34.55		23.65	30.96	89.16

3. *Add the 90-day accounts to your call list in their ranked order.* You now have a basis for making your collection calls for the month. You will probably find

that the accounts that have 90-day items also have 60-day items and 30-day items. When you call the account, your goal is to collect the entire delinquency, not just the 90-day items.

If this is the first time you have attempted to collect your delinquent accounts using this type of criteria, I suggest that you stop at this point and make the calls on your sheet. When you wish to refine your calling designation, go on to step 4.

4. *An option: Further refine your call list ranking.* When you wish to add a further refinement, you can examine each account that has a 90-day item and add in the other open items to further refine your account ranking. To do this you add the total for each column (30-day, 60-day, and 90-day) for each account, weighting the column totals as follows:
   - Multiply the 30-day column total by 1.0
   - Multiply the 60-day column total by 1.5
   - Multiply the 90-day column total by 3.0

As you can see, the older the amount, the greater its value. Figure 10 illustrates this concept.

The example in Figure 10 shows that when the accounts are ranked according to the 90-day column totals only, account 4529 is ranked first. But when all of the account columns are added using the weighted totals, account 4872 is ranked first. You can see that most of the accounts change rank when the 30-day and 60-day amounts are added. This example is very simple but it illustrates the concept of ranking accounts for collection calls. If you set your priorities in this manner, you have a good chance of bringing your collection problems under control in a short time.

Here is a summary of the process you should use to establish your telephone collection list.

1. Find all of the special handling accounts in your accounts receivable listing that are delinquent, or have large dollars in the "current" column.

Figure 10. Priority ranking of A/R listing.

```
OWEN  INTERNATIONAL          ACCOUNTS  RECEIVEABLE  DELINQUENCY  LISTING              PAGE 37
                            PERIOD ENDING:   SEPTEMBER, 30 1988
```

4529	GREEN & BARSTOW, INC	JANE BARSTOW	(714) 555-0921				
INVOICE	DATE	CURRENT	30-DAY	60-DAY	90-DAY+	TOTAL	②
S56742	05/23/88				94.30	94.30	
S62137	06/08/88				103.55	103.55	593.55
S78083	07/26/88			56.33		56.33	84.50
TOTAL				56.33	197.85	254.18	678.05

4654	HASKINS AUTOMOTIVE	ROBBIN SMITH	(213) 555-6840	**** SPECIAL PAYMENT PLAN PER H. OWEN ****			
INVOICE	DATE	CURRENT	30-DAY	60-DAY	90-DAY+	TOTAL	
S21219	02/03/88				678.00	678.00	
S21219	03/15/88				-100.00	-100.00	SPECIAL
S21219	05/02/88				-100.00	-100.00	
S21219	06/23/88				-100.00	-100.00	
S21219	08/26/88				-100.00	-100.00	
TOTAL					278.00	278.00	

4872	HORDCARE PHARMACY	JOHN HORDCARE	(714) 555-5533				
INVOICE	DATE	CURRENT	30-DAY	60-DAY	90-DAY+	TOTAL	①
P45222	04/13/88				23.86	23.86	202.83
P45223	04/13/88				43.75	43.75	
S78990	07/29/88			56.85		56.85	677.42
P79985	07/29/88			156.96		156.96	
P79986	07/29/88			237.80		237.80	
S89416	08/24/88		73.75			73.75	73.75
S97601	09/26/88	60.00				60.00	
TOTAL		60.00	73.75	451.61	67.61	652.97	954.0

5013	IMAGES, INC	KYLE BROWN	(818) 555 4700 EXT 336				
INVOICE	DATE	CURRENT	30-DAY	60-DAY	90-DAY+	TOTAL	③
S53510	06/15/88				83.95	83.95	26.85
S53510	06/30/88				-75.00	-75.00	
S68956	07/29/88			75.00		75.00	112.50
P71564	08/05/88		43.78			43.78	43.78
S85193	09/19/88	75.00				75.00	
TOTAL		75.00	43.78	75.00	8.95	202.73	183.13

5236	JONES HARDWARE	AMY HATHER	(213) 555-1200 EXT 12	*** ATTORNEY ACCOUNT ***			
INVOICE	DATE	CURRENT	30-DAY	60-DAY	90-DAY+	TOTAL	
S23490	02/09/88				95.75	95.75	
S25616	02/11/99				87.50	87.50	SPECIAL
S29745	02/16/88				150.60	150.60	
P32161	03/14/88				58.90	58.90	
TOTAL					392.75	392.75	

5549	KIELY & SONS	AMBER LOUIS	(818) 555-9800 EXT 43				
INVOICE	DATE	CURRENT	30-DAY	60-DAY	90-DAY+	TOTAL	④
P58901	05/31/88				180.96	180.96	92.88
P58901	06/10/88				-100.00	-100.00	
P58901	07/14/88				-50.00	-50.00	
S76292	07/18/88			23.65		23.65	35.43
P98342	09/30/88	34.55				34.55	
TOTAL		34.55		23.65	30.96	89.16	128.51

2. Find all large corporation, institution, and government accounts that are delinquent, or have large dollar amounts in the "current" column.

3. List all accounts that meet your telephone collection criteria, ranking them using weighted column totals.
4. Start making your collection calls.

The procedure for making an effective collection is described in Chapter 6, "Effective Telephone Collection Techniques."

Keeping Records

Record keeping is an essential part of the collection activity. The only point of contention might be how and where these records are stored. In the past, collection history cards were used during the actual collection period, and then stored in a customer collection history file. This made it easy to look up any customer file any time it was needed.

With the coming of the computer, some computer programmers decided it would be nice to be able to put the history file right on the computer with the customer account information.

In this way a collector could look up a delinquent account, make the collection call, and enter the information right into the computer file. I even worked with a system that allowed the collector to enter a promised payment date and the computer notified the collector if the payment was not made.

Sound great? Well, in my humble opinion we often try to computerize things that are much more easily done by hand. These computer systems have a great deal of "Gee Wiz" in them but very little practical help for the collector. I talk about this more, later in this chapter, in the section titled, "The Proper Use of the Computer in Collections."

I still advocate the use of telephone collection cards, or writing your actions right on the A/R aged delinquency listing. This gives you a progressive history of what action was taken on the account, and when. You can bind your A/R listings and quickly run through the history of any one of the accounts.

Personal Visits to Customers

There are two reasons that require you to make a personal visit to a customer's office or home. The first is for a collection call, and the second is for a public relations call. These two types of visits are completely different and need further explanation.

The Collection Call

The personal collection call was the main collection method when I started working in the credit industry. I use to spend all day, and some of the night, making personal calls on delinquent customers. Then someone got the idea that a collector could become more effective by calling customers on the telephone. I don't know who made the decision to convert to telephone collections, but it has made a radical difference in collection tactics and procedures. And it has increased the productivity of the collector three or fourfold.

Today, it is rare, or at least it should be, for a collector to make a personal visit to a delinquent customer. There are, however, times when you must go to the customer's home or office. In this section I describe the reason why you might make such a call, what to do before you go out, how to conduct yourself to protect yourself and your company, and what traps to watch out for.

WHEN AND WHY YOU MAKE A PERSONAL VISIT. There are times when you must visit the delinquent customer in person. The following situations might require a visit:

- To collect a payment at month end, when there is not enough time for the mail to reach you
- To verify location of merchandise
- To verify location of the customer

- To give personalized attention to a high account balance to show the customer that you feel the matter is very serious
- To review your records with the customer's, and it is more convenient for you to visit the customer than for the customer to come to your office

While these are not the only reasons, I'm sure you can name others, these illustrate some of the more general reasons that you might make a personal visit to a customer's home (consumer accounts) or place of business (commercial accounts).

WHAT TO DO BEFORE THE CALL. Before you visit the customer you must know exactly why you are going. You must have a stated purpose that can be quantified. You must know what you are going to bring back with you, or what problem will be resolved during your visit. You need to do all of your "homework" before you leave your office. If you are not completely prepared, you will be wasting your time and your customer's time.

HOW TO CONDUCT YOURSELF. Depending on the reason for the call, you might need to take care that you do not in any way break the law, or act in any way that might be construed as breaking the law. There are some areas that you must be aware of before you visit a customer.

Extortion. This is not something that you would generally think about, but when you make a personal visit to a customer you should be on the alert. Normally, when we think of extortion it brings to mind a gangster beating on some poor soul. The trouble with this connotation is that it only shows the far extreme.

Extortion is an act that makes the debtor feel he is being coerced into paying. If you are a large person, and the customer is much smaller, you could be accused of physical intimidation—which is extortion. It would be rare for this to happen if you conduct yourself in a friendly and businesslike manner, but you never know—you should always be on guard.

Slander. Slander is verbal defamation that might be heard by a third party. Verbal defamation that is heard only by the customer could, however, be construed as extortion. Watch what you say and how you say it when you are talking with the customer.

Be careful about mentioning the "delinquent account," or "delinquent invoices." State the facts as they are. "Our records show the invoice as unpaid." Choose your words carefully and never raise your voice to the customer or in any way become involved in a confrontation. If the customer becomes agitated, leave immediately.

Invasion of Privacy. If you go out to attempt to locate a customer who has "skipped," do not talk to anyone about the customer's relationship with your company. If you need to ask neighbors, or in the case of commercial accounts landlords, about the customer, simply say it is urgent that you find the person, that you have an important matter to discuss with them.

Assault and Battery. This is another case where we think of the extremes when we think of criminal acts. What do you think of when you hear the word "assault"? You think of someone getting "beat up," right? Well, assault is much less violent than that. Assault is putting the fear of injury, even if you only mean to scare them, into an individual.

The question is, How does the customer perceive the situation? If you do anything that makes the customer fear injury, you have committed assault—*even if you do not touch them.*

If assault is putting the fear of injury into a person, what is battery? Battery is intentionally inflicting an "injurious or offensive touch." Offensive means that it was made in a rude or insolent manner—even if no physical harm is involved.

With these definitions of assault and battery, how do you protect yourself against a lawsuit? Follow these guidelines:

- Never threaten a customer.
- Never touch a customer.
- Leave immediately if the conversation gets heated.
- When you discuss what will happen if the debt is not paid, simply state the facts—your attorney or collection agency will handle the matter.

Breaking and Entering. This should be a simple one. You know that you do not go out and break down doors, pry open windows, or in any other way "break into" a residence or office building—right? Again, our thinking goes to the extreme of the law.

Of course you should never use force to enter a customer's home or office. But what about going into a private office or a home when the door is standing open. Don't do it. Breaking and entering is passing the "plane" of a doorway that is not generally open to the public. You can go into a public area such as a reception room without an invitation, but that is as far as you can legally go without an invitation.

WATCH OUT FOR. . . . Here are some situations that you must avoid:

- Having a "heated" conversation with a customer
- Touching a customer, in what might be construed as an offensive manner
- Talking to any stranger about your relationship with the delinquent customer
- Entering an area that is not plainly marked as public, or is not generally open to the public during working hours
- Entering a home unless invited in by the occupant

- Leaving a note or message addressed to the delinquent customer about the delinquency when other people might be able to read it

These are some situations that you should always be on the alert for. If you always conduct yourself in a friendly and businesslike manner, you won't get into trouble. Watch out though—sometimes it is truly hard to maintain your cool, objective point of view—I know, I've been there.

The Public Relations Call

The other kind of personal visit is the one collection activity that I can say I truly enjoy. This can be a good experience where you will probably make new friends.

WHO GETS THIS TYPE OF VISIT? The public relations call is made on customers who have accounts with a high level of activity. Most of the time these will be the special handling accounts that I referred to earlier. Because these accounts have a large volume of activity, and because they are special by their very nature, or have been designated special by your company management, they do not receive the normal collection routine.

There are businesses, and in some cases individuals, who simply don't fit the normal categories in which we try to place them. Let's face facts; you are not going to sue a government agency and get much satisfaction. If you ever got to court, which I doubt you would, you would encounter more legal red tape than it would be worth.

In most cases it is not a money problem that keeps this type of account from being paid. It is a procedures problem.

If you deal with the government, or institutions like schools, school districts, and hospitals, you need to get to know the people who pay the bills. I talk about these special accounts later in this chapter, in the section titled, "Special Handling Accounts."

Skip Tracing

I have worked with some real "pros" in the skip tracing arena. The antics they went through to find a "lost customer," as they called them, were better than any TV private detective show. I have often wondered why television hasn't used a loan company or collection office of a business as a setting for a show.

These skip tracers that I have worked with have had more schemes than you could believe. The trouble with their skip tracing techniques is that they are now against the law.

The debtor now has rights, even when he or she is trying to avoid paying his legal debts. Remember that fact. It may not seem right, but it is still the law and you are the one who can get arrested for using illegal tactics to locate a lost customer.

The First Sign

The first sign of a skip is generally a disconnected telephone, or a returned letter marked, "Addressee unknown." If you call a delinquent customer and get a recorded message saying that the number is no longer in service, and that there is no new number—you have a skip. When mail is returned—you have a skip.

When you have reason to believe that your delinquent customer has skipped the area or has moved without notifying you, start your skip tracing procedure immediately. Time is important.

Tracing Consumer Accounts

Figure 11 shows the skip trace worksheet used for consumer accounts. You should have a sheet similar to this and fill it in immediately.

Use the following procedure to locate a skip:

Figure 11. Skip trace worksheet.

Skip Trace Worksheet

Date _____

Account Name _____ Account Number _____

Why Suspected Skip ☐ Mail Returned   ☐ Phone Disconnected

☐ Called Information. No new phone number. Area Codes Called: _____ _____

☐ Pulled Credit Application   _____ _____

    Contacted relative No Reason: _____

    Yes Result : _____

Contacted Employer   ☐ Still Employed   ☐ No Longer Employed

Contacted Spouse Employer   ☐ Still Employed   ☐ No Longer Employed

Comment: _____

Contacted ☐ Landlord ☐ Neighbors   Response _____

If homeowner :   Found house was for sale and contatced realtor.

Response _____
Sent form to locate latest address for customer vechicle.

Contacted the following:

☐ Banker   Response: _____

☐ Listed Customer as SKIP with Credit Bureau and asked for updated report.

Credit references:

_____

_____

_____

_____

_____

Final Action   ☐ Customer located   ☐ Account turned over to collection agency

Date action completed: _____

Collector : _____

---

1. Find the original credit application and call the "nearest relative."

    Ask where you can call the person. Use the consumer's first name and be very casual. If the relative asks what you want, you can say that you need to inquire about an urgent matter. Don't say anything more. If the relative won't give you a straight answer, you know you have a problem.

On the other hand, if he or she knows where the customer has moved, you may be told the number or that the customer will call you back. If a number where you can be reached is requested, give a number that is not answered using your company name.

2. While you have the credit application handy, write down the credit references and call each of them to see if anyone has a new address and telephone number. Say something like, "This is John Smith from Acme Company, and I just tried to contact our mutual customer Bill Jones on the telephone and found it had been disconnected. Do you have a current number for Mr. Jones?"

    Do this with all creditors listed on the application. If this brings up a blank, you should order a new credit report to see when the last inquiry was, and if possible, who made the inquiry.

3. Check the place of employment for all persons that are listed on the application, calling each company for an employment check. Do not mention why you are checking. If the person is still at the same place of employment, try calling the main switchboard and asking for him or her.

4. If you have a "cross street" (crisscross) directory, you can start calling neighbors to find out if they know what happened to the person. If you draw a blank at this point, it may be time to make a personal visit. Simply say that you know "John" and that you didn't realize that he had moved—nothing more.

The skip trace worksheet gives a number of places that you should call before giving up. Use the same informal approach when you talk with any of the people listed on the worksheet.

The time and money that you spend on a skip trace will depend on the amount outstanding. In some cases you will do a preliminary check and write the amount off to bad debt. In other cases you will do as much as you possibly can, and then turn it over to a collection agency for further action.

Tracing Commercial Accounts

Commercial customers do not generally skip out on their creditors. Most commercial businesses would find it hard to vanish into thin air. But there are some commercial accounts that manage to quietly fold their tents and move out.

I have had companies that appeared to be rather substantial simply close their doors and leave an empty building or office. On one of my more memorable moments I was *one day late* and encountered the IRS at my debtor's office. I wrote off a bad debt that day.

One of the reasons for getting the names and addresses of all officers or partners of a commercial account is to prepare for this type of situation. Armed with the names and addresses of the principals of the business, you can start locating them. If they too appear to have vanished, you can use the same skip tracing techniques you would use on a consumer account.

After you have done all that you can economically do in trying to locate a skipped customer, turn it over to an outside service.

The Use of Outside Collection Services

There are a number of good reasons why you should use an outside collection service. You may wish to use a collection agency or an attorney that specializes in collections. I do not think one is any better than the other. The key is to get someone that will work all of your accounts, and not just work the easy ones forgetting about the difficult ones.

Before you start using any outside service ask for references. You should call the references and ask the following questions:

- How long have they used the service?
- What type of accounts do they turn over?
- What process do they go through before turning an account over?
- What percent of the accounts they turn over do they get paid on?
- Is the service prompt in reporting account progress?
- Do they get paid promptly on recoveries?

These questions will give you a feel for the type of accounts the company is giving the service, whether the accounts are being worked before they are turned over, and other pertinent information.

Why Use an Outside Collection Service?

A qualified outside collection service can take the collection activity from the point that you exhaust your resources and capabilities. If you are able to go as far as an outside service can go, you may be spending too much on your inside collection activity.

If you have highly qualified collection people working your accounts, you may not need a collection service, but merely need the assistance of an attorney to handle the final legal matters. I believe that most companies do not need this level of collection expertise on the inside.

Banks and other financial organizations may indeed have a high level of collection expertise in their organizations. Their main product is the lending of money, and this makes it normal for them to have experts in retrieving their primary product. But companies that deal in nonfinancial goods should rely on the experts for this type of help.

When to Give Them the Account

You should be sending your accounts that reach the 90-day delinquency point and have had no action on the part of the customer, to the outside service.

Special Handling Accounts

Some accounts, because of their very nature, fall outside the normal collection process. Usually these customers are designated "special handling accounts." These customers do not receive any notices and are not handled as normal delinquent accounts.

Any account that falls into one or more of the following three categories should be handled as a special handling account.

1. Any large commercial account that your company management designates
2. Any government agency
3. Any institution such as a hospital, college, university, or school district

The Key Contact

When I talk about performing a credit check on this type of account, I say that each one should have a "key contact" designated. This is generally someone in the customer's accounts payable office.

Your key contact is the person that you work with to resolve any billing problems that make it difficult or impossible for the account to pay within the normal terms.

ESTABLISHING TELEPHONE RAPPORT. The first step in your contact with your key contact is to establish a good telephone rapport. You might make your first telephone call simply as an introduction, and as a time to schedule your next call. The key contact is generally a very busy person and you should acknowledge this fact in your first call.

In some cases there is a "best time" to make your calls. It may be a certain time of the month, or it may be a certain time of the day. This will vary from account to account, but you should ask about this in your first call.

MAKING A PUBLIC RELATIONS VISIT. The purpose for visits to special handling accounts is to get to know the people you talk to on the telephone, and just as important, for them to get to know you. It is much easier to pick up the telephone and call a friend than it is to call a stranger that you have never met.

You can also get to know the problems that the person has with your billing. As I have said before, sometimes it is impossible for these accounts to pay on time because your billing procedures are counter to what they need.

You should plan to visit these accounts at least twice a year. This keeps things friendly without getting too close. Also, you can't be away from the office too much or you won't get any work done.

CONTINUING A GOOD RELATIONSHIP. I have found that the more I worked to bring my company's billing into line with what these accounts needed, the better my relationship became with my key accounts. They knew I was on their side and that I worked to help lower their work load.

When I worked as a consultant, I did business with large corporations from time to time. I would establish my key contacts with each accounts payable department, and in many cases I was permitted to go to their office to pick up the check. I tried to do this as often as possible, not because the mail was slow, but because I found that when they knew I was coming by to pick up my check, they would get it processed on time.

I also made PR visits to these key accounts. At Christmas I brought a small box of candy for the department as a thank you to the people who had helped me. You must be very careful when you visit large corporations and government agencies to buy lunch or give gifts. I always asked if it was acceptable company or agency policy. If you do not ask, you may get yourself and your contact into trouble.

The Purchase Order

The central document for special handling accounts is the purchase order. This is the document that is used to control those folks who want to spend the company or agency's money. The people in accounts payable see themselves as the protectors of the company treasury. In many instances this is because they have been so designated by their management.

The purchase order is seen by many of these people as almost sacred in its importance. You must have a valid number, and your billing must be for the exact product or service the PO specifies.

There are some questions that you should ask as soon as possible regarding the purchase order and its role in the purchasing cycle.

The PO number—You should determine the most important numbers and/or characters in the PO number. In many cases government agencies are issued a block of numbers that have the same first ten to twelve numbers on all POs that they issue. You should ask your contact about the importance of the digits/characters in the PO number.

The requisition—A key question that you must ask is, "Can a product be shipped or a service rendered on a requisition number?" This may stop many late payments due to incorrect procedures by the people within their organization. If the company/agency rules require that the PO number be issued before purchase, you had better set up some type of procedure with your sales department to insure that this happens.

Are verbal POs acknowledged?—Along this same line you should find out if an order can be shipped before the hard copy of the PO is made up. Ask your contact if product can be shipped or service rendered on a verbal PO.

Who issues the PO?—You will also want to know who issues the PO. This can be helpful if your company has shipped the product, and the PO has not yet been issued—even if the company rules make this procedure acceptable. In many cases the accounts payable person cannot pay without the physical PO, and you are really the one who wants that invoice paid. So, you may have to be the one who "prods" the purchasing department to get the PO issued.

The Payment Cycle

Knowing the payment cycle for each of the special handling accounts is important. Knowing this all-important cycle of events can mean the difference between getting paid in 20 days or 90 days. The series of events that must happen before you can be paid varies from account to account but is as important as having the correct purchase order number on the invoice.

Figure 12 shows a typical payment cycle for a customer in this category.

While there are probably minor differences from customer to customer, the example shown in the figure will help you become aware of the general cycle that your product and invoice must go through before the invoice

Figure 12. Typical payment cycle.

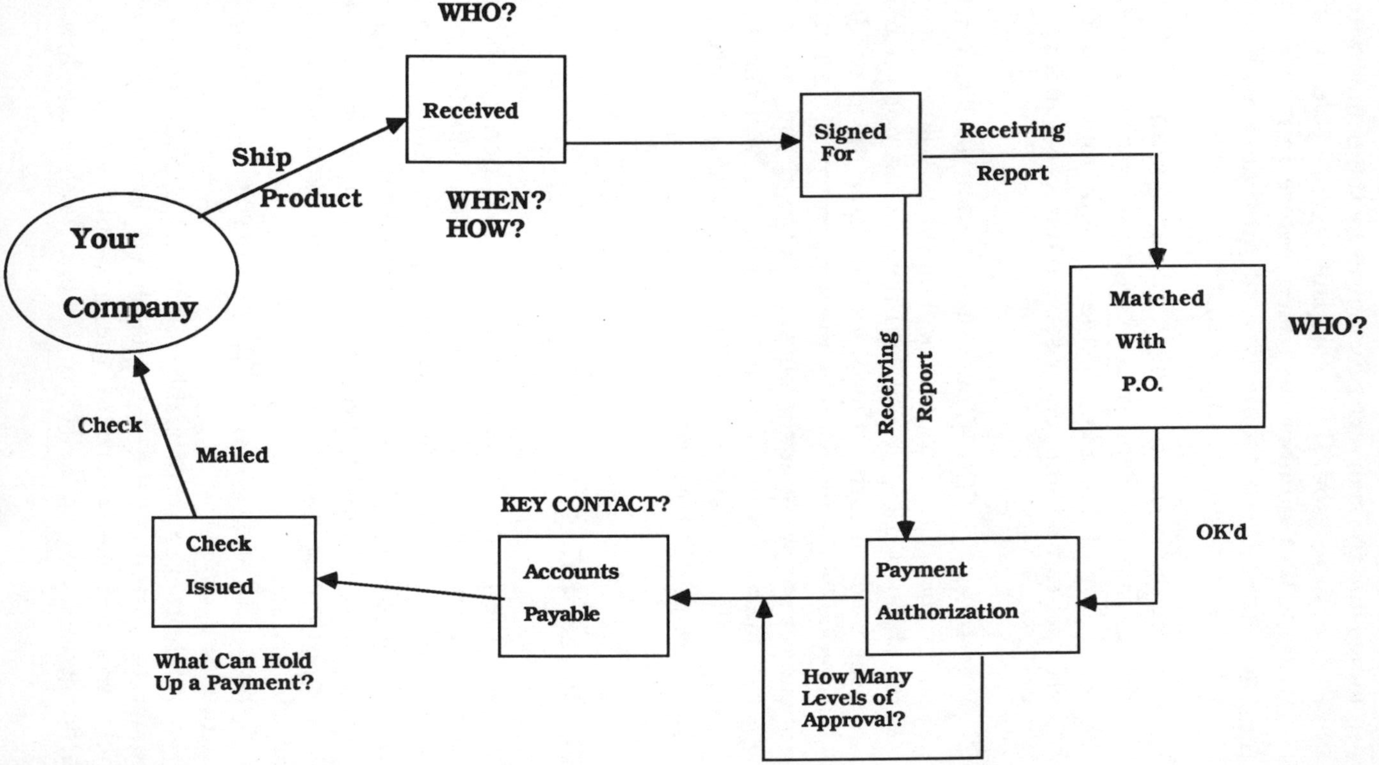

can be paid. The figure also lists the questions to ask about the payment cycle.

RECEIVING YOUR PRODUCT. The questions here are:

1. Are all goods received at a central receiving point?
2. Is a receiving report required before payment?
   —If so, who must sign it?
      Get the name and phone number of the person in the receiving department or the name of the manager of the department that ordered the goods.
3. Should the merchandise be delivered by a certain type of carrier?
   —Postal service
   —United Parcel Service
   —A courier/messenger service
   —Truck line
   —Your company truck
      You should know which of these is preferred by the customer. In many cases you should know which one is the easiest to check for delivery. I have spent many hours trying to prove that customers have received merchandise they claim was not delivered. It's not fun, so ship by the easiest carrier to prove delivery, if you are having this type of problem.
4. Who checks the receiving report/payment approval against the PO?
5. Who should receive it?
6. Who processes the payment?
7. Are there any steps left out?

It is very important that you write the events of the payment cycle on an account card listing each event and the person responsible by name, function, and telephone number.

A short story to illustrate this point. In the heyday of the American space program, IBM corporation did a great deal of business with the Johnson Space Center. The space center support program was a huge bureaucracy, and the process for getting invoice payment was very intricate and time consuming.

One of the collectors at IBM studied the process closely and finally developed a program that worked very well. It is too complex to give the details, but I can give you the general approach and you can understand his program.

- He defined the tasks that were needed for the space center to pay his invoices.
- He found the name and phone number of each of the people that had to process his billing.
- He visited each of these people and wrote down each of the procedures they were required to perform.
- He hand delivered every invoice to the first person on the processing task list.

His procedure from that point was to call the second person on the list in about two days and ask if he or she had received his billing from the person he had given it to.

If the answer was yes, he would verbally run through the process and ask the second person to pass it on to the next person. The process was repeated for each person on the processing list.

Now this may sound like a bit of overkill, but believe me it was the only way he could get any kind of timely payment on his outstanding invoices.

The point is that you should know the process that each customer uses to process your outstanding invoices. It can mean the difference between a 30-day payment and a 90-day payment. With the cost of money these days, your company needs its receivables paid as quickly as possible so it doesn't have to borrow additional funds for operations.

The Proper Use of the Computer in Collections

Before I talk about my philosophy of computers and their use in business, let me tell you a little about my background in the field. I entered the computer industry in 1962 as part of a team that was converting The First National Bank of Oregon to computer bookkeeping.

From that start I have worked in every area of data processing. I have sold computers, designed computer systems and coded programs, worked in both hardware and software engineering, toiled in the credit function, and scaled the corporate ladder to the executives suites of the corporate office.

I tell you this because, unlike many of my contemporaries, I do not believe that computerization is the answer to every problem. In fact I have seen many computer systems that have caused far greater work than the pencil and paper procedure they replaced.

One of the most striking is the system that scheduled conference rooms at a company where I worked. The office had five conference rooms that were used for various meetings. To use the rooms you had to sign up, listing your name and the time of your meeting in a "month-at-a-glance" calendar book. It was a very simple system and worked quite well.

Then one day someone decided that the "reservation system" should be computerized. In a building filled with programmers, it wasn't hard to find someone to do the task. When the task was completed and placed on one of our mainframe computers, it changed a quick, simple task to a procedure that could take fifteen minutes, if the computer was up and running. The computer strikes again! Having stood on my soapbox long enough, let me get to the point.

Tasks That Should Be Computerized

There are certain tasks that a computer does well and there are other tasks that it is not yet ready to handle. In the area of credit and collection the following tasks should be computerized:

Customer master record—This is a name and address file that contains all of the important information about your customers. What it contains is up to you. It can be nothing more than name and address, or it can contain items such as discount schedules, account representative information, and credit history.

Customer accounts receivable file—This contains the open billing information for each of your customers. With the coming of the personal computer (PC) into the business arena, there are many good programs at very reasonable prices that can quickly and easily computerize your accounts receivable system.

If you have, or can find, a front-end program that permits you to enter the order, bill the customer, and place the information into your accounts receivable file, that is even better.

But if you have to enter the customer billing information into the accounts receivable file by hand—do it, it will be worth the effort.

Payment processing—You should have a simple program that allows you to enter payment information into the A/R file and print out a daily payment report.
This program should perform the following tasks:
— Place the payment data into the A/R file if the invoice is not paid in full
— Remove invoices that are paid in full
— Print a report of the daily A/R payment transactions

A simple program like this is all you really need to keep track of the payments made against the A/R file.

File maintenance program—You need a program that permits file maintenance such as small balance write-off, or deletion of accounts that have a zero balance.

Accounts receivable delinquent list—You should have a program that lists your entire A/R file, by account, and spreads the open items by "current," "30-days" past due, "60-days" past due, and "90-days" past due.

To spread open items beyond 90 days is overkill. In the world of high interest rates, your company is losing about all it can when an account reaches 90-days delinquent. You need to resolve matters long before that.

You do not have to get fancy with your computerized A/R system to be effective. Watch out for the programs that try to do too much.

Tasks That Should *Not* Be Computerized

Computers do a great job on tasks that have to be repeated over and over. They also are great for storing and retrieving data. One of the areas that they are not good at is making judgments. Computers are not intelligent enough yet to help you select which accounts should be called today. There are systems available that try to do this, but I don't believe they are worth much. There is too much value judgment needed to make this type of decision, and computers are not up to it yet.

The other area I believe computers are not quite ready for is the on-screen note taking systems. I work with a PC every day, and I have a program that is an on-screen calendar/notepad/tickler file. I have yet to use it—it takes too much time. I'm sure any medical or dental office will back me on this—computers are too slow when you are typing to make an appointment and you have two other lines holding. With the coming of the windowing environments, these systems may become usable, but I have not found one that saved me any time—yet.

Chapter 6

EFFECTIVE TELEPHONE COLLECTION TECHNIQUES

THERE ARE two underlying reasons for your collection efforts:

1. Bringing the customer account current
2. Keeping the account as a customer

Both of these reasons are equally important until management has decided that your company no longer wants to do business with the customer. Does this mean that you can then harass the account? Not at all. Harassment of any kind, at any time, is generally self-defeating.

Keep this in mind when you use your most powerful collection tool—the telephone. By applying the proven telephone collection techniques explained in this chapter, you enhance your effectiveness as a collector. You will also find that your job activities will develop into a pleasant, personal, rewarding experience.

If you are an experienced collector, study these techniques to see where you can improve your collection efforts. If you are new to the job, memorize this program and you will become an effective accounts receivable collector and company marketing representative.

The procedure for calling a delinquent account is broken down into three phases:

1. Planning the call
2. The collection call
3. Follow-up tasks after the call

It is important to remember that all three phases are necessary for your success. If you skip the precall planning before you make the call, or skip the follow-up after the call, you will not be as effective as you could be. Even if you think parts of the plan are unnecessary—try them, you will be surprised at the results you get.

Phase #1: Planning the Call

In Chapter 5 you studied the overall collection program and you learned how to determine whether an account was sent a notice, a letter, or required a personal telephone call. When you determine that an account requires a telephone collection call, you must do some homework before you pick up the telephone.

There are eight steps in your precall planning research.

STEP 1: Check Payment Record

Your department records should show the previous payment record for all accounts. If it doesn't, start collecting this information now. Look at the payment record to determine whether collection activity has taken place in the past.

STEP 2: Check for Past
Collection Efforts

Review the collection actions and responses from previous collection activity (if there has been any) to get a good feel for this customer's attitude.

You need to know:

- When the last collection call was made. Was it last week, or was it last year. This makes a big difference in your overall approach to the customer.
- The reason for the call. Was it the last in a long series of collection calls, or was it one call a year ago that brought immediate payment. The answer will determine the overall emphasis you give in your call.
- The final disposition of the collection call.

STEP 3: Check Current
Billing for Accuracy

If you are new to this collection department, you should start investigating the billing cycle and the validity of the company billing. You must know if this delinquency could possibly be your company's fault.

I was called recently by one of my creditors, and the first words were, "We're going to be in your neighborhood tomorrow, and we'd like to pick up your payment." This was after I had sent two letters telling the creditor that my checks had cleared the bank but had not been credited to my account. I had even gone to the trouble of giving cancellation information from the three checks that had been deposited by his company.

The collector knew nothing about my letters and he backed off quickly, but I still resent the call. That company has gone down in my eyes. If this is its general collection policy, it will lose many good customers in the years to come—even if its product is superior (which it is).

STEP 4: Determine the Key Contact

If you are a company that sells your product to other companies, sometimes it is hard to find the "decision maker." By the decision maker I mean the person who is responsible for paying your outstanding bill. It is difficult, and sometimes very embarrassing trying to collect the bill from the wrong person.

Even if you have to go back to the original contract or invoice to find this information, it may save you hours of frustration. This is especially true if the account is a large corporation or government agency. Call the sales representative, or the sales desk, to see who they deal with. But if all else fails, ask for the "accounts payable department."

STEP 5: Plan Your Strategy

The next step in the precall planning is to decide how you are going to approach this customer. If you have an account with a long history of delinquency, you will approach the collection call differently than one who has never been delinquent.

Review the types of personalities that you might encounter as explained in Chapter 3. If you understand this information, you will be able to control the collection situation. This knowledge can be the difference between success and failure. Study it until you can place your customers into a classification.

Based on your research of the account history, you should be able to come up with a strategy. You should know how you are going to approach the collection situation.

If this is an account that is new, or you cannot find a collection record, there is only one valid strategy; ask why the account is not current, and ask what you can do to help the situation. Using this approach, you will avoid any embarrassment if it turns out to be your company's fault. You also assume that there is a problem that you can help resolve. Your resolution may indeed be to come up with a payment plan.

There are two basic strategies that you can use. The first is based on no collection history, or very little delinquency over a long period of time. Here you assume that there is a problem, and that you and the customer can work out a solution that will benefit both parties.

The second strategy is based on your own experience with the customer. You know what happened during the last call and you know exactly what was promised. You can go into this type of call much bolder and much firmer if the customer has not fulfilled part of the agreement.

STEP 6: Predetermine Your "Bottom Line" Payment Plan

Normally, you want to get the entire past due amount paid with one collection call. This is the "best case" scenario. But the real world says that you probably will not get the entire payment due on this one call, so you need to decide what amount you will accept.

If this account has a history of delinquency, you can use past collection activity as a rule of thumb. If you are new to this account, you should temper this with your understanding of the last collector's effectiveness. If the last collector who called this account was very effective, you can pretty much accept the history as valid. But, if the last collector was not very effective, and you can see where long spread-out collection plans have been used, you might want to attempt a tighter collection plan.

STEP 7: Prepare Your Questions

Fact-finding is the process of asking questions that help you determine why the customer is delinquent. When you have gathered enough facts, you can sell the payment plan that you have put together; or you may have to modify your plan to fit the new set of facts.

You should prepare a list of questions that you can use for all collection situations. The purpose is to find the real reason the customer has not paid the bill on time. There are two criteria that you should consider:

1. The question must be open-ended so that the customer can respond with meaningful information— not just yes or no. Ask questions that allow the customer to do the majority of the talking.
2. The questions should require the customer to give reasons why the bill has not been paid. This will give you the information you need to sell your payment plan. It may also give you information that will allow you to modify the plan to fit new circumstances.

STEP 8: Consider Your Opening Statement

Your opening statement should be a statement of fact. "Hello, this is John Jones from Owen International. Our records show that you have not paid invoice ABC1234, and that it is now 60 days past due." This is a truthful statement in all cases. Your records, right or wrong, indicate that invoice ABC1234 has not been paid.

If you have talked to the customer before, and they have acknowledged the past due amount and have given you a promised payment date that has passed, you might open with, "Hello, Mr. Smyth, this is John Jones from Owen International. I haven't received the payment you promised on the twentieth."

Your opening statement should be brief, clear, and to the point. No matter what your strategy is, stop after the opening statement and allow the customer to respond.

This may seem like a complex series of steps to go through before you talk to all of your customers, but you will find that the process will become second nature and as you develop you will need less and less preparation time. But if you are a new collector, or you are new to this group of accounts, you should go through this series of preparation steps before each call. It will save time and effort in the end.

Phase #2: The Collection Call

You have researched the history of the customer, you have written down a list of questions that will allow the customer to tell you why the payment is delinquent, and you have determined your strategy and bottom-line payment plan. Now you are ready to make the collection call.

There are ten steps in a successful collection call.

STEP 1: Get to the Right Person

Ask for the person by name if at all possible. If you haven't been able to determine the right person, ask for accounts payable, or if it is a small company, ask for the person in charge of accounts payable.

STEP 2: Identify Yourself and Your Firm

The way you open your call is vitally important. During the first 10 to 15 seconds, you will set the tone for the entire call. During this time you will be doing most of the talking. You should be pleasant, and relaxed, but leave no doubt that you are serious about collecting the overdue account.

If you are new, and you want to write your opening statement, that is perfectly acceptable. Make it short and to the point. You might say, "Hello, my name is Susan Allen from ABC Corporation."

STEP 3: State Your Reason for Calling

After you have given your name, and your company if you feel it is needed (the person on the other end of the phone doesn't know you well enough to put together you with your company), you state your reason for calling.

If you haven't talked with this person before, you might say, "I am calling about your account. There are two invoices that are over 30 days past due." Use the opening statement that you prepared while you were planning the call.

STEP 4: Pause

This next step is the most powerful, and most misunderstood part of a successful collection call. After you have given your name, company, and reason for calling—stop talking.

There is an adage in the sales world that goes like this, "Give the prospect your pitch—then shut up. First person to speak loses."

There is a power in silence. Sales professionals use it all the time. And this collection call is a sales situation, we have already talked about that. So try it—a pause after you give your name, company, and reason for calling can cut minutes off the call.

This pause is formally referred to as the "strategic pause," but it is so powerful it is often called the "pregnant pause."

A strategic pause requires the least effort on your part. But it works wonders because it shifts the burden of con-

versation to the customer and gives him or her a chance
to volunteer an explanation. I use this tool everytime I can,
and it has worked wonders for me. Try it—you'll like it.

Never let the pause go more than 10 seconds. If there
is no response in that time, ask your first question.

STEP 5: Ask the Prepared Questions

The facts that you have learned from the customer in answer
to your strategic pause tell you about the situation and
about the customer's personality. The way he or she has
answered, as well as the information given, allows you to
make judgments about the person you are dealing with.

Your first question should be open-ended and should
give the customer a chance to tell why the payment is past
due. Keep asking the questions until you are sure you have
found the real reason the account is not paid.

There are two processes going on when you ask questions. The first is speaking and the second is listening. Your
questions must be clear enough that the customer does not
misinterpret them, and you must be an expert listener when
you finish the question.

You must learn the art of listening. This is not something that most of us do very well. Your effectiveness as a
collector is determined by your ability to be a good listener.
It is essential that you become an expert listener.

Here are the keys to good listening:

1. Limit your own talking. You can't talk and listen
   at the same time. When you are talking you are
   not learning. Limit your talking to short, appropriate questions that steer the conversation toward
   your objective.
2. Think like the customer. The problems and needs
   of the customer are real, important, and relevant
   to the collection situation.
3. Ask questions. Ask questions based on what the
   customer is saying. Steer the conversation with
   your questions.

4. Don't interrupt. Wait until the customer has finished before you start talking. A long pause does not mean the person is finished. He or she might be thinking about the way to tell you the real reason for nonpayment.

5. Concentrate. Focus your mind on what is being said. Practice shutting out distractions. When you can learn to put all your consciousness into your conversations, you will become more effective.

6. Take notes. This helps you remember important facts. But don't try to take down the entire conversation—be selective. Write down key points that will help you put together strong questions. When you try to write down the entire conversation, you find that you get left behind.

7. Listen for ideas . . . not just words. As the conversation progresses, you will see a pattern start to unfold. You have written down key points, and you now have the "big picture" to respond to.

8. Listen for the overtones. Listen for the subtle voice inflections that tell you more than the words. Start to listen between the lines. The way something is said can have more of an impact than the words themselves. If you don't believe this, start listening to the evening news. You will find that everything that is said is carefully spoken to give the "right" point of view.

9. Answer occasionally. Give a short response occasionally. A simple "Yes, . . ." "I see, . . ." "Certainly," shows the customer you are there and listening. Be careful not to overdo it, because this can cause confusion.

10. Turn off your personal thoughts. This is difficult to do at first. With practice you will be able to turn off your personal life and become totally attentive to the person on the other end of the telephone.

11. Prepare in advance. You should have questions that you have prepared, as I have said. You can

use these questions as the basis for your conversation. You may have to do some rephrasing, but at least you have a foundation to start from.

12. React to the answers NOT the customer. Never let what the customer says get to you personally. If the person says something derogatory about you, and you think it is over the limit, break off the conversation and hang up. If this happens, you should write down the exact conversation as closely as you can remember it and give it to your manager.

13. Don't jump to conclusions. Listen to the complete explanation before you draw a conclusion. Don't mentally jump into the middle with unwarranted assumptions.

14. Practice listening. If you are going to become an expert listener, you must practice. Make your conversations with family, friends, and business associates your classroom. It will pay off by enhancing your ability to hear what people are really saying, not just the words they are using.

STEP 6: Determine Any Objections to Payment or Reason for Delinquency

During the question and answer session you are finding out why the customer hasn't paid the account current. Using this information, present a payment plan that you can live with, and that you feel the customer can meet. This may not (and should not) be your "bottom-line" payment plan.

If the customer feels that he or she cannot meet these terms, you will be given the reasons. Sometimes you will get a counterproposal, or some objection to payment.

STEP 7: Set Aside Problems and Get a Commitment to Pay Invoices That Are Okay

Try to set aside objections and go on to a meeting of the minds. Objections are almost always postponements—reasons for not bringing the account up-to-date now.

There are three things you must do to overcome objections.

1. Determine specifically what the customer is objecting to.
2. Get an agreement on the parts of the plan he is not objecting to.
3. Work out an agreeable solution to the objections.

For example, the customer owes $1,250 on six invoices that are over 30 days delinquent. Your plan proposes:

- $300 in 15 days
- $600 in 30 days
- $350 in 45 days
- All new invoices paid current

The customer may say, "I can't make the $600 payment that soon." You can answer, "Okay, what about the other two payment schedules?"

You have set aside the one objection without jeopardizing the entire plan.

The customer may state that the merchandise for two of the invoices was returned. You determine that they were given to the sales representative two weeks ago, and the credit memo has not been issued yet.

You can set aside the objection to those two invoices and get a commitment for the remainder.

**STEP 8: Come Back to Problem
Items and Determine What Action
to Take on Each Problem**

If the customer raises objections that require action on your part, you should go through them, and their impact on the payment you are to receive, before you end the call. You should detail the action that you must take, and the action you expect from the customer.

**STEP 9: Present an Overall
Plan of Action**

You can then present the overall plan in a recap. This is what you have just agreed upon. It must be spelled out before you end the call.

Present it in the following form:

- Actions that you are to take and the results
- Actions that the customer is to take with dates of payments included

STEP 10: Close the Call

After you have summarized the agreed upon payment plan, thank the customer and close the call.

The steps given here may not always occur in this order, in fact every one may not be apparent in every call. But these are the steps that occur whether they are visible or not.

Phase #3: The Follow-Up

After your call you have three things to do.

STEP 1: Record Your Notes

The first thing you do is record the call in reasonable, understandable notes. Next week you may get that promotion to the New York Head Office and some brand new collector may have to follow up on your accounts.

**STEP 2: Take Any Action
You Committed to Take**

Take the commitment that you promised. Ask the sales representative where the merchandise is from the two invoices. He or she may say that it was given to the warehouse and has a returned items slip to prove it. Whatever it takes, get the credit memo for the customer.

STEP 3: Confirm Your Action to the Customer by a Return Call or Letter

When you have taken the appropriate action you promised, you should write a letter to the customer confirming what you have done, and confirming the payment plan.

This is one of the components of the most powerful tools you have against delinquent accounts. It is also one of your company's most powerful tools for customer satisfaction.

Always remember—you are an extension of the sales department.

Chapter 7

CREDIT GRANTING PROCEDURES

Y OU CAN use this chapter as a guideline for writing your company credit and collection procedures manual. If you find that the policy statements and procedures fit you well enough, you can use the chapter as it stands. It started as a credit and collection policy manual for one of my clients. The only things that I have removed are direct references to the company. In place of its name, I have used "the company."

165

Policies and Procedures

This chapter describes the policies and procedures that are to be used when investigating credit histories, determining credit status, and communicating this information to the prospective customer, or the established customer.

Credit Policy Statement

The credit policy of the company should be consistent in all respects with overall company policies, goals, and objectives.

Customers should be given a written statement disclosing all credit terms and performance requirements relative to the conduct of their business with the company.

The credit/collection department should be positive in all its relations with customers, the business community at large, and other departments within the company.

The credit/collection department should recognize the company's sales and marketing objectives. While closely adhering to specific credit-granting policy, the credit/collection department should cooperate with the sales department to accept new credit business likely to become a source of additional, on-going profit to the company.

The credit/collection department must be prudent to protect the company's accounts receivable investment, and should maintain a collection program that is firm but fair, flexible but consistent.

On a monthly basis, the credit/collection department should inform company management of the dollar investment and the aging of the accounts receivable file, with information essential for evaluating the performance of the collection program.

Definition of the Credit Department

The credit/collection department should include all personnel directly involved with accounts receivable activities, including supervisory, line management, and staff personnel. Indirectly involved personnel, such as accountants, bookkeepers, and others should be made aware of the credit/collection department to the extent that their own activities can help or hinder it.

Included within the credit/collection department are all customer account files, invoice files, and other records normally maintained by the department or for which it is responsible.

Functions of the Credit Department

The credit/collection department should be responsible for performing the following functions on a regular basis:

1. Gathering and evaluating credit information, and making credit decisions for new credit customers
2. Reviewing and adjusting credit limits for established customers
3. Collecting monies due the company
4. Applying customer payments to appropriate accounts
5. Helping with customers on all billing and/or collection problems
6. Making billing adjustments to customer accounts
7. Maintaining all customer account files
8. Maintaining security of the invoice files

Credit Granting

This section describes the policy and the procedures that the credit/collection department is to use during the credit investigation and the credit decision.

Credit Granting Policy

In keeping with company credit policy, the credit/collection department should assume the responsibility to:

1. Gather information
2. Evaluate the information
3. Accept or reject credit applications
4. Set credits limits or credit lines for each credit application accepted.

The department should complete such evaluations within an established time period, such as 48 hours. When it is impossible to establish the credit standing of any application within the normal time, the credit/collection department should notify the sales department to allow for contingency planning.

The credit/collection department should handle any application for credit limit reevaluation, or the reopening of dormant accounts, on the same timely basis as a new account. Any credit limit reevaluation request which exceeds a predetermined figure established by the company, such as $200, $500, or any other amount, should require a new credit report from an outside report agency.

All credit information should be gathered in a straightforward, direct manner. A credit gathering and reporting agency should be contacted and used as the primary source of credit history information. At no time should a company employee use misrepresentations or other deceptive methods to gather credit information from a credit reporting agency or to directly check with banks or other trade sources.

Information Gathering

From a credit investigation standpoint, there are four distinct types of customers.

1. Individuals buying personal (consumer) products
2. Individuals doing business under their own name on a small scale, or as a proprietorship or a partnership that has just started in business and does not have a credit history
3. Local businesses with established credit histories

4. Large major corporations and businesses that are well-known and financially stable, government agencies, and institutions such as schools and hospitals

Credit history information about these customers can be acquired from the following sources:

1. Information about individuals can be obtained through the local credit bureau, or by directly checking with the references listed on the application.
2. Local businesses may be checked out through the local business credit exchange, or by directly checking with references listed on the application.
3. Major corporations do not require a normal credit check in most cases, but beware of assuming financial stability simply because of high visibility. Check with your local agency before making any credit judgment if you feel there is any question about the company.
4. Government agencies such as state operated hospitals, school districts, and local, state, and federal agencies cannot be checked out in the normal manner. The procedure for credit checking these institutions and agencies is discussed in detail in a later section.

SOURCES OF CREDIT INFORMATION. The following sources of credit information are to be used when investigating credit applications:

Local credit bureaus: In most cases local credit bureaus limit their credit gathering activities to individuals. There are, however, local credit bureaus which will gather and give out information on both individuals and businesses when these customers are located in the immediate community.

Local industrial or business credit exchange bureaus: These local credit exchange bureaus have been established to credit check commercial business accounts only and do not deal with individuals. If you are unable to locate a commercial credit exchange, you may contact the National Association of Credit Management, head-quartered in New York City. This organization is the largest of its type in the United States and has over 37,000 members in cities throughout the country.

Dun and Bradstreet: The Dun and Bradstreet Reference Book: The names and ratings of almost 3 million businesses located in the United States and Canada are contained in this book. They are arranged alphabetically, by city or town within their particular state or province. The book lists manufacturers, wholesalers, retailers, business services, and other types of businesses buying regularly on credit terms.

Dun and Bradstreet: The Dun and Bradstreet Report: Dun and Bradstreet offers a complete reporting service similar to that which is offered by other commercial credit reporting exchanges.

A complete listing of services available through Dun and Bradstreet can be obtained through your local D & B representative listed in the telephone book.

Direct checking: Because some businesses and individuals do not have a credit history listed in the local credit bureau or business exchange or are not listed in the D & B Book, it is necessary to check directly with references that they give to validate their payment history.

There are, however, many problems with this type of credit checking. They are:
— Time consuming
— More costly than a consolidated check through a local credit bureau

— Inaccurate or incomplete information because the person filling out the credit application will give you only good references
— CAUTION: Some states prohibit the direct checking of credit references by independent companies.

Financial statements and balance sheets: These particular instruments should be limited to use with companies or transactions that exceed $5,000. A financial statement and a balance sheet will give a credit manager necessary information to make a decision regarding the financial health of companies requesting credit. There are many excellent books on financial statement and balance sheet analysis, which can be found at your local public library.

Major corporation/government agency credit application statement: When a major corporation or a government agency wishes to establish an open account with the company, the procedure for checking the credit history of that company or assuring yourself of a timely payment is not the same as with other customers. The process is not one of checking past payment history to determine whether the company can pay you or will pay you on a timely basis, but rather, determining the company's or agency's paying procedures so that your company can submit valid, relevant data on the invoices to assure timely payment.

Large national and multinational corporations and government agencies are usually very rigid in their invoicing requirements. It is essential that a company doing business with this type of organization know the invoicing and payment requirements and routines so that it can follow them and assure payment of its own invoices on time. The exact information needed and the exact routine for checking one of these companies or agencies is shown in greater detail below.

The information needed for a credit check varies with the type of account to be checked. Listed below are some of the common requirements for basic types of accounts.

The Individual. Figure 13 shows an example of a credit application that can be used for an individual.

Complete the following information:

1. Credit amount or line requested
2. The first section of the application including social security number and driver's license number
3. Names and addresses of other partnership
4. At least one bank reference, with the name of a bank officer who will serve as a contact, if possible
5. At least two local credit references, not to include
   — A major oil company credit card
   — Mortgage companies
   — Mastercard or VISA cards
   — Other national credit cards
   — Credit unions
6. The bottom section of the credit application including signature and date

Granting credit to an individual based on information from references given by the customer is a poor policy. A complete file history, such as that given by the local credit bureau, is the only valid criteria on which to base a credit decision. References given by the customer will usually be the best he or she has.

To administer an efficient, consistent general credit policy it is essential to have effective front-end protection. It is not good policy to deny a credit limit simply because a customer has no credit history. On the other hand, it is also not good policy to grant credit limits to persons who have abused their credit privileges in the past. Obviously, the only way to get an accurate history is to gather all the information possible.

Figure 13. Consumer credit application.

Owen International, Ltd.

Credit Application

Credit Amount Requested: _____

Name _____ Soc. Sec. No. _____

Address _____ Apt # _____

City _____ St . _____ Zip Code _____

Employer _____ Address _____ Phone _____

Title _____ Years on Job _____ Salary _____ Weekly   Bi-Monthly   Monthly

Bank _____ Branch _____ Ck Acct # _____

Address _____ City _____ Sav Acct # _____

Credit References:

Company	Type of Credit	L = Loan O = Open account R = Revolving	High Credit	Current Balance
_____	_____		_____	_____
_____	_____		_____	_____
_____	_____		_____	_____
_____	_____		_____	_____

I /we understand the following and will abide by your company regulations:

1. If granted credit, I/we agree to pay all invoices within 30 days of invoice date.
2. It is agreed that I/we will pay 1.5% per month which is 18% yearly, for all past due balances.
3. It is agreed that my/our account will become C.O.D. if I/we fail to pay invoices within the above stated terms.
4. My/our financial condition is satisfactory and I/we can meet all financial obligations.
5. There are no lawsuits or judgments against me at this present time. If I/we default on payment of any outstanding valid invoices I/we agree to pay attorney and/or collection expenses.

I /we make the foregoing application for credit for the purpose of obtaining merchandise on an open account basis.

Name   Date

_____   _____   ☐ Primary   ☐ Co-signer

_____   _____   ☐ Primary   ☐ Co-signer

_____   _____   ☐ Primary   ☐ Co-signer

Local Businesses. Figure 14 shows an example of a credit application that can be used for commercial accounts.

This application asks for the following information:

1. Credit line requested.
2. All information in the first section of the application.

Figure 14. Commercial credit application.

Owen International, Ltd.
Credit Application

Credit Amount Requested: _____

Company Name _____ Telephone _____

Address _____ City _____ St. ____ Zip _____

Type of Bus. _____ In Bus. Since _____ At Above Add. Since _____

Business Structure: ☐ Corporation ☐ Partnership ☐ Individual Ownership

Name of Partners or Corporate Officers, if applicable.

Name	Title	Address	City	State Zip

Bank References (at least one)

Bank _____ Branch _____ Acct # _____

Address _____ City _____ St . ____ Zip _____

Bank _____ Branch _____ Acct # _____

Address _____ City _____ St . ____ Zip _____

Trade References (at least two)

Firm Name	Address , City, State, Zip	High Credit

I understand the following and will abide by your company regulations:

1. Notify Owen Internaltional, Ltd. of any changes in ownership of our company.
2. If granted credit, our company agrees to pay all invoices within 30 days of invoice date.
3. It is agreed that our company will pay 1.5% per month which is 18% yearly for all past due balances.
4. It is agreed that our account will become C.O.D. if we fail to pay invoices within the above stated terms.
5. Our company financial condition is satisfactory and we can meet all financial obligations.
6. There are no lawsuits or judgments against me at this present time. If our company defaults on payment of
   any outstanding valid invoices we agree to pay attorney and/or collection expenses.

I make the foregoing application for credit for the purpose of obtaining merchandise on an open account basis.

_____ _____ _____
           Name   Title   Date

3. Names and addresses of at least two principals in the company (partners or corporate officers).
4. Bank references, with the name of an officer who will serve as a contact, if possible.

5. Trade references (two or more).
6. Is a purchase order required to validate each purchase?
7. Who can sign for product, and what are their limits, if any? (List on the back of the application.)
8. Signature (by partner or officer only) with title.

For major corporations and government agencies:

1. Name and exact billing address. See Figure 3 (key account profile) for an example of the credit application used for this type of account.
2. If a subsidiary or division of another company, name of parent company; or, if a subagency of another government agency, the full relationship should be shown.
3. Telephone number of the accounts payable department or agency.
4. Key contact (a person) in the accounts payable department.
5. The following information regarding purchase orders:
   —What is a typical purchase order number?
   —What are the most meaningful or significant numbers within the purchase order for expedited payment?
   —Does the company/agency issue blanket purchase orders?
   —Are verbal purchase order numbers to be accepted?
   —Can a requisition number be accepted as a firm order? Or is a purchase order and PO number required to validate an order?

CREDIT APPLICATION LOGGING PROCEDURES. All credit applications can be logged in and handled in the following manner, or a similar one established by the company:

1. Enter into a credit application log. Figure 15 shows an example of the credit application log.
2. Assign a log/security number.
3. Place application in a pending call file.
4. Call file into appropriate credit exchange or credit bureau (at least twice a day).
5. Place in pending callback file.
6. Receive callback from credit bureau and make credit decision.
7. File in the company credit application file.

Evaluation of Information

The amount of time and money spent to check on any credit application should be in direct proportion to the credit amount requested. Obviously, a credit application requesting a $10,000 credit limit should be evaluated in more detail than an application requesting a single purchase of $100 that is to be repaid at $10 a month.

When you receive a credit history file from a reporting agency, consider the following information:

1. *Name and address* (social security number if an individual's file). This information obviously verifies that this is the correct file.
2. *In file since.* This line reveals how long the person or company has been conducting credit business in the local area. The date given will indicate when a credit file was established at the reporting agency. If this is a relatively short time (less than two years), ask if there are files available from other credit bureaus, as the customer may have moved into the area recently. In dealing with an application from someone new to the area, ask the credit bureau to check with the foreign bureau (city of applicant's last residence) and transfer the file information into its local office.

IMPORTANCE OF INFORMATION Various types, or levels, of credit are granted by business establishments. For ex-

Figure 15. Credit application log.

Credit Application Log

Firm Name	Appl. Date	Appl. Number	Accept	Reject	Pending	Credit Request	Credit Author.	Ltr Sent	Cust Number	Credit Date

ample, most commercial credit helps to finance another company's business operations, while consumer credit generally finances personal items and, sometimes, real personal necessities.

Commercial accounts. Consider all the following items in making a commercial credit granting decision:

1. *Type of business.* Knowing the type of business can be very important. Here are some questions to consider about the applicant and its industry in general: What are the trends of the industry?
   - Is it a glamour industry?
   - Is it upswing?
   - Is it a dying industry?
   - Is it a new industry, with room for growth?
   - Is it an overcrowded industry?
   What is the applicant's position in the industry?
   - Is it a new company, or an individual going into new business?
   - Is it an established company or at least an established entrepreneur?
   - Is it one of the industry leaders, or a very large company?
   Where is this company in its industry?
   - Mainstream of the industry?
   - A unique company?
   - What makes it unique?
   Is this a positive factor?
   Is this a negative factor?

2. *Relationship of product to customer's revenues.* What effect will your company's product or service have on your customer's ability to produce revenue? How crucial are you to your customer's operations?

3. *Time in business.* Stability is the key here.
   An established individual or company?
   A start-up operation?

If it is a start-up business, how is it capitalized?
If an individual, does he or she have any other
sources of income? Watch start-up operations closely.

4. *Consider the item purchased.* The past purchase and
   good payment on a piece of business equipment, a
   car, a boat, or a personal item does not necessarily
   have any bearing on the manner in which your
   payment will be made, and therefore should not be
   a major factor in the credit decision you make. Your
   product or service may be unsecured; that is, there
   may be nothing with residual value that could be
   repossessed or taken back to cover the debt if it is
   not paid. It may be a product or service with lower
   priority and therefore lower the place on the payment scale. When looking at high credit previously
   granted, look for credit granted for products or
   services similar, if possible, to your own company's.

5. *Previous credit given.* When the average or normal
   amount of previous credit has been determined for
   the customer in question, the following questions
   should be answered if the customer has requested
   a larger amount of credit than that previously given:
   • Does your product directly affect the customer's
     revenue potential or expenses?
   • Has the customer been awarded a large contract?
   • Is the customer's business growing rapidly?

6. *Payment history.* It is important to consider who the
   customer has been paying as well as how he or she
   has been paying. Consider these questions:
   • Does the customer pay suppliers similar to your
     company on time?
   • If there is a poor paying record, who is it that is
     paid slowly?
   • If the customer is on a COD basis with some firms,
     why? Remember, some companies and individuals
     do not grant credit, and therefore COD is a nor-

mal condition. Also, the customer may have requested cash terms, or may not have applied for credit. Not all trade references are credit references; don't assume COD status to be a negative. Ask the bureau to investigate if there are any questions.

7. *Bank balance and history.* A bank balance must be consistent with the amount of credit requested. A customer with a low 3 (from $100 to 300) checking account requesting a $1,000 monthly credit line would be suspect. Another item to watch for is a history of NSF checks. No matter how high the average balance, customers with a past history of NSF checks must be considered closely before being granted a credit approval—of any size.

Consumer accounts. Consider all the following items in making a consumer credit granting decision:

1. *Income.* It is important to consider amount of income that a person has on a monthly basis and the source or sources of that income. A person may be employed, and be paid regularly on a monthly basis, and/or may have income derived from various other sources. These might be income producing properties, savings accounts, annuities, alimony and child support payments, and social security or retirement benefits.

   You evaluate the applicant's income to answer the first of two questions that must be answered in the credit investigation: Can the person pay? The income is a very good indicator of his or her ability to pay. If at all possible, all income listed on the credit application should be verified.

   All the other questions are asked to answer the second question: Will the applicant pay according to the terms of the contract?

2. *Employment.* Employment listed should be verified with the company, and the time on the job should also be verified, if possible. If it is not possible to verify stated income, verifying position within the company will give a good indication as to whether the income stated is valid or not.
There are two reasons for having employment listed: the first is to cross-reference job level with stated income; the second is to verify stability by determining the time on the job.
3. *Living accommodations.* Another indicator of stability is a person's living accommodations. Generally speaking (this is not always true on an individual basis), a person who owns a home is more stable than one who rents, and a person who rents is generally more stable than one who lives with relatives. Another indicator of stability in this area is the time at present address, and the time at one previous address at least.
4. *Dependents.* These are listed only as means of assessing the person's personal expenses. It is simply a fact that it takes more to feed a family of five than to live alone.
5. *Bank accounts.* The person with a checking account with $100 in it is not as stable or does not show an ability to pay as a person with a checking account with $1,000 in it and a savings account containing another $1,000. These are just other indicators of stability and ability to pay.
6. *Telephone number.* For years there has been a saying in the credit business: No phone—no loan.
7. *Credit history.* The credit history of an individual should be viewed in much the same way as explained in the previous section on commercial credit.
8. *What is being purchased.* If there is any question about the individual's ability to pay, or desire or willingness to pay, the item being purchased should be considered carefully. It would be a far more prudent credit

decision to loan $15,000 on a home with a fully secured first deed of trust than to loan $15,000 on an unsecured personal note. Not all credit decisions are this cut-and-dried, but if there is any indication that the person will not or can not pay, the item being purchased must be considered in the credit decision.

Making the Credit Decision

A credit limit is the dollar amount of your product or service you will agree to provide a customer, within a specified period (generally a month), without reviewing his credit history or requiring cash payment.

The company will establish its own credit limit policy. Shown below are the parameters that have been established by one small business services company as the basis for establishing credit limits. If the company uses a similar schedule, the following parameters might be minimum conditions for each indicated credit limit:

1. *$50 limit.* Must have a bank account which has been open at least six months. Must have maintained a high 2 (from $60 to $99) balance with no returned checks. Must have no bad information listed in a credit bureau history file.
2. *$100 limit.* Bank account—one year, low 3 rating, no bad checks, no bad credit history.
3. *$200 limit.* Bank account—one year, low 3 rating, no bad checks, satisfactory credit history of one year with two other firms, high credit of at least $150.
4. *$500 limit.* Bank account—two years, med 3 rating, no bad checks, satisfactory credit history of two to three years with at least two other firms, high credit rating of at least $350.

5. *$750 limit.* Bank account—three to five years, high 3 rating, no bad checks, or, bank account—one to two years, low 4 rating, no bad checks, satisfactory credit history of three to five years with four other firms, high credit limit of at least $500.
6. *$1,000 limit.* Bank account—three to five years, med 4 rating, no bad checks, or, bank account—one to two years, high 4 rating, no bad checks, satisfactory credit history over five years, high credit limit of at least $1,000.
7. *Above $1000, or unlimited.* All major companies, all government agencies, any company with a stable business history over five years that the credit manager or a company official considers a good risk.

If the credit manager decides to grant a customer a credit limit outside the guidelines established by the company, he or she should document the reasons on the back of the credit application.

When a credit limit has been established for a customer, a letter stating the credit limit and explaining credit terms and conditions should be sent to the customer as shown in Figure 16. If credit has been rejected or a lower limit has been established than the customer requested, this should also be confirmed in writing, as shown in Figure 17.

If the credit history of any customer is such that the credit manager feels it is unwise to extend credit at all, or at least unwise to extend credit at the level the customer requests, he or she should contact the customer by telephone and explain the reasons, allowing the customer a chance to explain any unsatisfactory past.

Reevaluating Credit Limits and/or Account Status

In the course of normal business, it is necessary to reevaluate credit limits, sometimes raising them and sometimes lowering them as individual cases warrant.

Figure 16. Credit acceptance letter.

Owen International, Ltd.
_____

44 City Parkway South
Suite 2200
Anaheim, California 92808
(509) 238 - 9000

March 2, 1989

Higgins Machinery Company
7854 Vermont Street
Irvine, Cakifornia

This is to inform you that your credit application has been approved and your account is now open at Owen International, Ltd.

You will be sent a statement of account around the first of each month showing all open invoices as of the last working day of the previous month. We will appreciate your checking the invoices that you have received against your monthly statement to help insure complete accuracy.

Our terms are net 30 days of the invoice. It is understood that delinquent accounts are subject to suspension until brought current. We urge our customers to avoid this inconvenience.

If you have any questions regarding the status of your account, or specific charges appearing on your monthly statement, please do not hestitate to contact me.

Please note that we are opening your credit limit at $500.

If at any time in the future you feel that this amount will not be sufficient to cover current monthly charges, please contact this office for a reevaluation, rather than over-extending your approved limit.

It is a pleasure to serve you.

Sincerely,

Frank Lee Speeking
Credit Manager

At the request of either the sales department or a customer, a credit limit may be reviewed for adjustment. On a monthly or other basis, the accounts receivable file should be reviewed and all accounts with billing over 60-days past terms should be considered for lower credit limits or a COD status.

Figure 17. Credit rejection letter.

Owen   International,   Ltd._____

44 City Parkway South
Suite 2200
Anaheim, California 92808
(509) 238 - 9000

December 24, 1988

Kent Baker
12 St Cloud Drive
Newport Beach, California 92672

Dear Mr. Baker,

During our recent investigation for your request for an open account
with Owen International we found that there were items on your TRW
credit file that keep us from being able to grant your request for
a credit line.

If you have any questions regarding these items, or would like to
review your TRW credit file, you may send a copy of this letter to
TRW in Orange, California and they will send a copy of your file
free of charge.

If there is erroneous information on your report, and you can clear
it off, please feel free to reapply to Owen International for a line
of credit.

Yours truly,

Frank Lee Speeking
Credit Manager

For a higher credit limit:

1. Pull customer file and review the original credit
   bureau file
2. Review the customer's payment history with the
   company

3. Get a new credit report if considered appropriate
4. Use your own history and latest credit bureau report as a basis for raising a credit limit

For lower credit limit:

1. Monthly, review all accounts with invoices 60 to 89 days delinquent
2. Review accounts that habitually pay during this time period for possible action

Any time a change is made in the status of a customer's credit limit, the change should be transmitted as follows:

1. The customer should be notified via a telephone call and/or a letter (see Figures 18 and 19).
2. An account change sheet, or some other reporting device used by the company, should be made out for your own department records, and to use for informing other departments within the company.

Release of Credit Information for Outside Requests

Many companies prefer to check directly with trade references rather than use a credit bureau for their credit checking. It is common practice for companies to exchange credit history information.

However, this practice can be dangerous and has led to lawsuits. Creditors have been sued because the customer felt information was given out that was wrong and misleading. Any information given the company should be restricted to the indisputable facts as listed below, and no interpretation or rating of the account should be allowed.

Credit history information should never be given out directly to incoming calls; they should be handled as follows:

Figure 18. Reevaluation of credit limit—up.

Owen International, Ltd.
_____

44 City Parkway South
Suite 2200
Anaheim, California 92808
(509) 238 - 9000

July 15, 1988

Hector Garcia
1409 Front Street
Santa Ana, California

Dear Mr. Garcia,

Your request for an increase in your credit limit has been reveiwed
and I am happy to say that it has been approved.

Thank you very much for the prompt payments on your account during
the last year and a half. You are one of our much appreciated
customers.

As we discussed, we are going to raise your limit from $500 a month
to $1000 a month. Under normal circumstances we would not raise a
limit this much at one time. But because your case is special, and your
payments have been so prompt, we are happy to accomodate your needs.

Thank you again for your business. If you have any questions regarding
your account in the future please feel free to contact me.

Sincerely,

Frank Lee Speeking
Credit Manager

1. Get the company name, the name of the individual
   requesting the information, the telephone number,
   and the name of the customer in question.
2. Tell the caller you will call him or her back.
3. Determine the opening date.
4. Review the past history and any collection history
   of account in question.

Figure 19. Reevaluation of credit limit—down.

Owen International, Ltd.

44 City Parkway South
Suite 2200
Anaheim, California 92808
(509) 238 - 9000

July 12, 1988

Dale M. Warner
2219 S.E. 68th Ave
Oakland, California 94566

Dear Mr. Warner,

After a thorough review of your account, Owen International is lowering your credit limit from $1000 to $600.

When you have maintained a current account at the $600 limit for a period of one year, you can apply again for a higher credit limit.

It is important that you realize that our company requires prompt payment on all billings. Please refrain from paying your monthly billing on a late basis or we will be forced to place your account on a C.O.D. basis.

If you have any questions about this decision, please feel free to contact me and we can dicuss it.

Sincerely,

Frank Lee Speeking
Credit Manager

5. Verify the company's existence and phone number by looking it up in the phone book or calling information. When you have validated the company, return the call and give the following information only:

A. Date account opened.
B. Last sale, if known.
C. High account balance.
D. Amount owing, and how much is current, 30-day, 60-day, and 90-day-old;
E. Your company's credit terms.
F. Approximate average paying cycle for this customer.
G. If the account has been turned over to an attorney or a collection agency, state this as a fact.
H. Do not give a rating for the account. You have given enough information to the inquiring company for them to determine their own rating.

Chapter 8

COLLECTION PROGRAM PROCEDURES

Y OU CAN use this chapter as a guideline for writing your company collection program procedures manual. If you find that the policy statements and procedures fit you well enough, you can use the chapter as it stands. It started as a credit and collection policy manual for one of my clients. The only things that I have removed are direct references to the company.

This chapter describes the policies and procedures that are to be used for the collection of delinquent accounts— through to the write-off of accounts as bad debts.

191

The Collection Program

The company's collection program is not simply a money retrieval system. Instead, it is an integral part of the total sales process. The main objective of the collection program is to develop customer relations through which the company will recover its delinquent receivables as quickly and economically as possible, while encouraging the formerly delinquent customer to patronize the company with future good business.

The collection program should use straightforward, direct tactics in all efforts to collect past due accounts. No employee should use misrepresentation or deceptive methods to collect or attempt to collect past due accounts. When any attempt is made to collect past due accounts, regardless of the medium, the purpose of the attempt should be clearly stated to the customer.

The collection program should be a consistent program where all customers—large and small—are treated with the same respect. Any exceptions to the standard program should be fully documented, with reasons and corroborations clearly stated.

Accounts Receivable File Analysis

The procedures in this section are to be used to analyze the accounts receivable file for delinquency status and for work load assignments.

FILE ANALYSIS. To analyze the A/R file accounts, do the following:

1. Review all invoices 90 or more days delinquent, by the following method:
   a. Run an adding machine tape of all invoices over 90 days old, by account total.
   b. Review the tape for the largest account totals.

     c. Determine the total "dollar amount" repre-
sented by the top 20 percent. (If there are two
hundred accounts with invoices over 90 days
old, the top forty would represent 20 percent
of the total.)

2. Review 60-day delinquent invoices, using above
method.

3. Review 30-day delinquent invoices, using above
method.

4. Compare the adding machine tapes of the 30, 60,
and 90 day account totals, determine:

     a. How many accounts are represented on all three
listings?

     b. How many in at least two?

     c. What is the aggregate total of the top 20 percent
of each column? (If an account is in the top 20
percent in more than one column, only count
it once.)

The above analysis will give you the starting number
of telephone calls that should be made. In commercial
collections, it is safe to say that this 15-20 percent of the
total accounts that have been isolated as the "top dollar"
accounts will represent 75 percent of your total delinquency.

WORK LOAD ANALYSIS. In a normal small or medium-size
business, each full-time collector should be able to handle
between 450 and 900 accounts, depending on the work
load distribution within the department. Here is a "normal"
breakdown:

1. Full-time collectors with no responsibilities other
than telephone collections can handle up to 900
accounts.

2. Collectors who must handle credit applications, post
customer accounts, handle problem accounts and
billing discrepancies, handle file maintenance along

with other duties, would have their ability to call greatly reduced.

Assessing the work load is a difficult problem. The following guidelines can be used:

1. "Single item" accounts, such as: time payment, revolving charge, rental or lease billing payments, can be called at the rate of 50 to 60 calls each day. Seventy-five percent of these calls will be completed, which means that 750 to 900 effective calls per month can be made by a collector (with no other responsibility assigned) working this type of account.
2. Commercial accounts with 2 to 10 items or transactions per month, can be called at the rate of 35 to 40 calls each day, with the same 75 percent effectiveness factor. This means a collector assigned the responsibility for only calling accounts can handle 500 to 600 accounts monthly.
3. Accounts with over ten transactions per month greatly reduce the number of calls a collector can handle.
4. Additional duties will also reduce the number of calls a collector can make. A time study should be done (see Figure 20) to determine exactly how much time is available for telephone collection activity.

A parameter can now be established for the top dollar limit in the collection letter program, using the following information:

1. The lowest dollar figure of the "top 20 percent accounts."
2. The results of the time study which will reveal the amount of time available for the collector to make telephone calls.

Figure 20. Time study sheet.

TIME STUDY SHEET   **Daily Activity**

8:00 to 8:30	12:00 to 12:30
8:30 to 9:00	12:30 to 1:00
9:00 to 9:30	1:00 to 1:30
9:30 to 10:00	1:30 to 2:00
10:00 to 10:30	2:00 to 2:30
10:30 to 11:00	2:30 to 3:00
11:00 to 11:30	3:00 to 3:30
11:30 to 12:00	3:30 to 4:00

The number of "top 20 accounts" will tell you how many telephone calls should be made each month. The results of the time study will indicate how many telephone collection calls the collection department can make. These two figures will allow a parameter to be established for the top dollar limit of the collection letter program, and the bottom dollar limit for the telephone collection program.

Collection Letter Notice Program

The purpose of the letter/notice program should be to effect the collection of small-dollar, low-volume accounts. The collection department should have a system that will determine which accounts are to receive collection letters. By the end of each month, the collection department should prepare a listing (manually, by computer assistance, or by automatic computer program) of the accounts designated to receive delinquency notification.

FIRST DELINQUENT LETTER. Accounts designated to receive the first delinquent letter should meet the following criteria:

1. Have current billing, 30-day, and 60-day delinquent billing only. Any account with older billing should be handled by another collection method or medium.
2. Total delinquent billing should not exceed the established criteria. Any account which exceeds the established criteria in overdue billing should be contacted by telephone.

When regular statements are sent out, all customer accounts that meet the criteria listed above should be sent the first collection letter. (See Figures 4 and 5 for an example.)

SECOND DELINQUENT LETTER. All accounts that received a first collection letter at the beginning of the month, but still have unpaid billing by the fifteenth of the month, should be sent the second collection letter, (see Figure 6 for an example) by the twentieth of the month.

COD LETTER PROGRAM. Accounts that meet all of the following criteria should be sent the COD letter (see Figure 7 for an example) in lieu of the normal statement:

1. Have received both the first and the second collection letters within the last month, or a telephone collection call, or a personal visit, yet have not responded to the collection effort
2. Have invoices that are at least 60 to 89 days delinquent and unpaid
3. Have a total account balance of less than (dollar amount to be determined by the company)

If the company's accounts receivable file is computerized, it should be a simple matter to establish a procedure for identifying those accounts which are to receive collection letters each month. "Flagging" programs can be written in several ways, depending on the type and sophistication of the computer involved. In any case, the COD letter should normally not be a computerized letter, but should be individually typed. By doing this you will not cause the customer to feel that he or she is dealing with a computer, and it will be more difficult to ignore the collection effort.

After the letters have been prepared by the typist, they should be returned to the collection department. Review them with the updated A/R file to assure that no payment has been received on the accounts in question before sending out the letters.

Note: Before sending out COD letters check carefully to assure the validity of doing so. A quick check with the sales department (if applicable) could save a bad situation and prevent creating an unhappy customer. Be assured that the "month end A/R closing" presents the entire picture of the customer's account and not just part of the billing.

Telephone Collection Program

The telephone collection program is meant to handle high-dollar, high-volume accounts, or any account specified for special handling by company management. The telephone collection program is an extention of the sales program, and at all times should be administered as such.

The purpose of the telephone contact is to establish rapport with the delinquent customer, and to get a firm commitment of payment as soon as possible.

The telephone collection program should be conducted continuously during the month, with a minimum number of telephone collections calls (the number to be established by your needs as explained above) made each day.

Each month, a listing of potential telephone collection program accounts should be prepared, to include:

1. The *special handling* accounts regularly called (see "Exceptions to the Normal Collection Process," in this section for a full explanation)
2. Any account with a single invoice of (dollar amount to be determined by the company) in any column
3. Those accounts which have received collection notices within the last month but have delinquent balances in excess of letter program criteria

Handle the accounts which are listed for the telephone collection program as follows:

1. Before making the initial contact with any customer, make a short check (a couple minutes at the most) into the account's past history, billing validity, and other pertinent items.
2. Determine the right person to contact.
3. After reaching this "right" person, state name, company name, and reason for the call.
4. Determine reason for nonpayment and answer any complaints or objections to making payment.

5. Get confirmation of intent to pay, or,
6. Establish what must be done by the company (if anything) before payment will be made.
7. Repeat any agreement for action, whether by the company or the customer.
8. Thank the customer and close the call in as positive a manner as possible.

A written confirmation to the customer is necessary if:

1. A payment plan with more than one payment has been agreed upon.
2. A payment plan that extends beyond two weeks has been agreed upon.
3. Any action is required of the company's personnel. The action taken should be documented, and the terms of the agreement should be restated to the customer in the letter of confirmation.
4. Any time the collector feels there is a chance that the customer will not fulfill the agreement he or she made for payment of the delinquent invoice.

Personal Visits to Customer Locations

Personal visits should be made only when it is necessary to establish a closer relationship with a customer. These visits should be limited, and used only as a last resort, except for the regular visits to large commercial and government accounts.

Personal visits should be used as part of the overall collection program in the following instances:

1. A potential skip, within a reasonable distance from the office.
2. Any account with a 90-day plus delinquency that exceeds the company's established parameters, and telephone collection techniques have been unsuc-

cessful in resolving the problem. This visit, with the appropriate salesperson, if possible, should be made to attempt a final collection effort before assigning the account to an outside service.

3. All large commercial and government accounts should be visited on a regular basis (once or twice a year), to establish close working relationships between the company's collection personnel and customer's accounts payable personnel.

Before making any personal visit, contact the customer by telephone and attempt to resolve the situation over the phone.

1. Enter private areas only at the invitation of the customer. This applies to private residences, a personal/private office, or any area other than a public waiting room or an area normally visited by the general public during regular business hours.

2. Do not attempt or imply any physical action or violence.

3. Do not attempt or imply any verbal abuse or coersion.

4. If at any time, the customer requests you, the collector, to leave, do so immediately.

5. If at any time, the customer seems uneasy or seems likely to become abusive or violent, leave immediately.

6. At all times, conduct yourself in a businesslike manner, being polite but firm in all the collection activities with the customer.

Attorney/Agency Accounts

Delinquent accounts should be turned over to an outside collection agency only as a last resort in the collection activity. All accounts that are turned over for collection must have gone through the normal collection cycle and should have received:

1. Delinquent notices, or
2. Telephone collection call, and
3. A letter stating that the account will be handled on a COD basis, and
4. A letter stating that the account will go to an outside collection agency or attorney for further action. Figure 8 shows an example of an agency/attorney letter.

When an account is turned over to an outside collection source, all monies outstanding must be turned over, not just the 90-day delinquent items.

The company will use the following system for maintaining records relating to accounts that have been turned over to an agency. Credit/collection personnel will monitor the collection activity of these accounts. A basic account collection record will be maintained that contains the following information:

1. All invoices, debit and credit memos, and other account entries.
2. All background data of the company collection activity, including such items as copies of telephone collection activity records and COD letter(s)
3. Customer's trade name (where applicable)
4. The company account number
5. The attorney/agency identification number
6. Collection file number
7. Amount of customer account submitted for collection
8. Reason for referral—such as, bad check, normal collection procedure, or skip

Accounts submitted for outside collection activity shall be handled as follows:

1. Verbal follow-up to confirm receipt of the file within one week.
2. Written acknowledgment from the outside agency or attorney within 30 days of submission.
3. A written update of all collection activity must be received from the agency or attorney at least every three months. This shall include:
   A. Summary of the dollars collected to date
   B. Summary of the collection activity
   C. A written statement of uncollectibility for those accounts that have not been collected, or which seem to be uncollectible in the near future (90 days), or which seem too expensive to pursue

Exceptions to the Normal Collection Process

Some accounts, because of their very nature, fall outside the normal collection process. Such accounts are designated special handling accounts. These accounts do not receive any notices and are not handled in the company's normal collection routine.

All accounts which fall into one or more of the following categories below shall be designated SPECIAL HANDLING ACCOUNTS:

1. Any large commercial or industrial account that company management designates in writing to the credit/collection department as a special handling account
2. Any local, state, or federal government agency
3. Any other account that has been designated in writing for special handling by company management

Each of the accounts that is assigned as a special handling account shall be contacted at least once every month that there is an outstanding balance on its account record. This contact shall be either by telephone or a personal call. Handle all such accounts by using the following routine:

1. Establish a special handling collection card for the designated accounts
2. Establish a customer key person to be contacted regarding all billing matters for each account
3. Contact the key person once a month regarding
   A. All invoices 30 or more days past due
   B. All large invoices
4. Follow the procedure below in all such telephone contacts:
   A. Give the purchase order number or identification number that is relevant to the customer
   B. State the invoice number
   C. Ask if the invoice was received
   D. Ask if there are any questions or problems regarding this particular invoice

If there are no problems with the invoice in question, get a commitment for a payment date. If the accounts payable person, or the key contact with whom you regularly speak, says that the invoice cannot be paid within the current month, find out the exact reason and attempt to resolve the issue, getting the payment at the earliest possible date.

Keep a collection log for each special handling account. This log is similar to the telephone collection account log. Enter the following information:

1. The date of each contact (personal or telephone call)
2. The name of the person contacted
3. Any problems, or other relevant information

Skip Accounts

A skip account is any customer with an unpaid balance that moved without notifying the company. A customer shall be classified as a potential skip if the following occurs:

1. Mail is returned to the company marked MOVED—NO FORWARDING ADDRESS or NO SUCH PERSON AT THIS ADDRESS.
2. The telephone has been disconnected with no referral number.

When a customer is classified as a potential skip, take the following action immediately:

1. Complete the top portion of a skip trace work sheet. Figure 11 shows an example of this form.
2. Call the telephone company Information and try to get a new telephone number in the local area.
3. Pull the credit application and review the following items:
   A. Consumer: Relative listed. There should be a name, address, and telephone number.
      Commercial: Officers or partners listed. These individuals can and should each be called.
   B. Employment for individual or spouse. The company can be called to verify current employment. Attempt to reach the individual on the job. At no time shall you attempt any collection activity if you reach an individual on the job. Ask for a number where he or she can be reached, or ask for a place where you can meet.
   C. Is the consumer renting a home or apartment? If so, contact the owner of the house or apartment manager. If the consumer is buying a house, find out who listed the house, who sold it, and other helpful information through the real estate company.
   D. Social security number and driver license number, and a car license if available. Use this data to locate the vehicle through the state vehicle agency.
   E. A bank account number and an officer's name if available. Call the bank to verify that the account is still open.

F. Other credit references. Call all references to determine the current address in their files. Contact the collection department of the references. Tell the collector your situation. Attempt to get all current information you can about the account.

4. Contact the following personnel within the company who might be helpful:
   A. The sales staff
   B. Order desk
   C. Service or field personnel

5. Contact the local credit bureau or commercial credit exchange and give them the following information:
   A. List the person/account as a potential skip.
   B. Get an updated credit report from each of the creditors who is listed on the credit application. (When direct checking is practiced, do this directly with the credit reference.) Have the credit agency do a credit update for you, to get any new credit source names and addresses.

6. Complete the actions on the skip trace work sheet.

When the skip trace work sheet has been completed, and the customer is still missing, immediately refer the account to an outside collection service for action. Time is the key in finding skip accounts.

Bankruptcy

Customer bankruptcy may occur from time to time. The company's interests are best served by proper handling of such situations as they occur. To respond properly as a collector, you must know the rules.

According to the law, to be adjudged bankrupt, an individual (a corporation is an entity under the law, and is considered an individual) must not have done any of the following:

1. Concealed, removed, or permitted to be concealed or removed, any part of his or her property, with intent to hinder, delay, or defraud creditors for any of it, or made a transfer of any of his or her property, fraudulent under the provisions of the act
2. Made a preferential transfer
3. Suffered or permitted, while insolvent, any creditor to obtain a lien upon any of his or her property through legal proceedings or distraint and not having vacated or discharged such lien within 30 days from the date thereof, or at least 5 days before the date set for any sale or other deposition of the property
4. Made a general assignment for the benefit of creditors
5. Insolvent or unable to pay their debts and willing to be adjudged a bankrupt.

Normally, bankruptcy notification comes from the court. If you have reason to believe that a customer is bankrupt, but have not received court notification, attempt to claim the company's share of the assets, by following the procedure below:

When no bankruptcy number is available:

1. Get the bankruptcy number from a customer who is claiming bankruptcy. If the customer cannot or will not give the number, ask if an attorney is handling the matter, and get the telephone number. Call the attorney and get the bankruptcy number.
2. If the customer is unable, or unwilling to give you a valid bankruptcy number, do not handle the account as a bankruptcy. When the customer claims bankruptcy, but is unable, or not willing to give you the number, record the time, date, person spoken to, and all other pertinent information on the collection sheet.

3. Contact the bankruptcy court in the customer's local area and identify the customer by name and address, and ask the court for a bankrupcty number.

If the court is unable to give you a bankruptcy number, handle the account as a normal delinquency.

When a bankruptcy number is available:

1. Complete the top portion of the customer bankruptcy form.
2. Call the bankruptcy court in the customer's local area and confirm the number.
3. If the company is not listed on the creditor list, ask for the required paperwork to file as a creditor.
4. Ask the court clerk to send a bankruptcy notice.
5. When the bankruptcy paperwork arrives, complete the form and submit it immediately.
6. When the debt has been registered with the court, process the account as a bad debt write-off, giving bankruptcy as the reason, or if applicable, have the customer reassume the delinquent balance by writing a new contract.
7. If the customer does not reassume the debt, make no further contact with the debtor about invoices, or any other debts incurred prior to the bankruptcy date.
8. Handle any monies received from the court as described in "Recoveries" section of this manual.

Bad Debt Write-Offs

This section describes the methods for handling bad debt write-offs. All bad debt accounts are to be processed in accordance with this procedure. All invoices classified as bad debt must meet one or more of the following criteria:

1. Is billed to a customer who has been declared a bankrupt by the court. The invoices in question

must be dated prior to the bankruptcy date. A statement of claim must be filed with the court for all outstanding debts written off in this manner.

2. Has been declared in writing as uncollectible by an outside collection agency or attorney.
3. Is classified as "too expensive to collect" by an appropriate member of management.
4. Has a total account value of LESS THAN (dollar amount to be established by company) and is assumed too expensive to collect.
5. Is billed to a customer who has been declared a skip. Any account with a balance GREATER THAN (dollar amount to be established by company) must have the written statement of an outside collection agency or attorney.
6. Is declared as uncollectible within a reasonable period of time by an appropriate member of management.

Note: Merchandise (products or services) not delivered to, or picked up by, the customer cannot be written off as a bad debt. Such merchandise must be credited according to company procedures.

Every account written off as a bad debt shall have an individual bad debt write-off file established, to include:

1. Invoices that were written off
2. Total amount written off
3. Date transferred to bad debts general ledger account
4. All collection activity work sheets
5. Authorization for write-off

Recoveries

All monies received from debtors for debts previously written off as bad debts shall be applied to the recoveries general ledger account, in accordance with company policy.

NSF/Account Closed Checks

All checks returned by the bank stamped NSF (Not Sufficient Funds) or Account Closed shall be handled as follows:

1. Log in the check.
2. Contact the customer and proceed with regular collection activity.
3. If the customer cannot be located, process a skip trace work sheet, as outlined in the section.
4. Allow the check to be replaced by money order, cashier's check, or cash only.

Chapter 9

CASH APPLICATION AND INVOICE SECURITY

Y OU CAN use this chapter as a guideline for writing your company credit and collection procedures manual. If you find that the policy statements and procedures fit you well enough, you can use the chapter as it stands. It started as a credit and collection policy manual for one of my clients. The only things that I have removed are direct references to the company.

This chapter describes the policies and procedures that are to be used when applying customer cash payments, and for invoice security.

Cash Application

This section describes the aspects of cash application.

Cash Application Policy

All remittances from the company's customers should be applied to the appropriate customer account, on the day received and in the manner specified (or anticipated) by the customer. Any remittance credit made to a customer's account in a manner other than directly specified or expected by the customer must first have the customer's approval.

All remittance advice paperwork should be kept in accordance with basic procedures outlined in this section. Any cash application made to a customer's account other than that specified by the accompanying paperwork should be noted on the paperwork. Any remittance received without remittance advice should be handled in accordance with procedures outlined in this section.

The unapplied cash payment mode should be used only as a last resort.

Verification of Invoice Payment and Logging

The application of all customer remittances should be verified by attached remittance advice from the customer. The application of cash to the customer account should be documented in a cash application journal if you are hand posting the remittances. If you are using a computer program to post the remittances, the computer should print a cash application report for the transaction day.

All checks received as customer remittance should be handled as follows:

1. Verify check and remittance advice (if included) to the account as listed in the accounts receivable file including:
   A. Name and account number
   B. Amount of check and remittance advice to account's open items
2. A remittance that matches the account exactly should be listed on the cash application journal and entered onto the file.
3. List all remittance that matches the account exactly on the cash application journal and process them according to your company procedures.
4. Store all remittance advices in an envelope, or appropriate container, marked with the application date. These containers are to be retained as determined by the company records retention policy.

Exception Payments

Not all payments sent in by customers match the amount, or invoice numbers on their account. Any customer payment that does not match the accounts receivable file is considered to be an exception payment. All exception payments are to be handled using the following procedure:

1. Invoices dated after the latest accounts receivable closing date should be verified directly against the open invoice file.
2. A remittance that is over or short (amount to be determined by company) the amount of the account, shall be posted and the difference written off to the appropriate general ledger account.
3. Any remittance that has erroneously excluded or included tax should be investigated for validity. If tax exclusion is proper, the tax amount must be

credited out. If tax has been included on an account that your records indicate is not taxable, contact the customer to determine why, and what future action must be taken.

4. Any remittance that exceeds the limits of paragraph 3 above, if it cannot be reconciled with the company's records, requires contact with the customer.

5. Upon confirmation of proper application of the remittance by the customer, a written notification should be made as follows:
   A. Account name and the account number
   B. Date of conversation
   C. Person giving authorization of application
   D. Manner of application
      This information should be stored with the remittance advices for the day.

6. If customer contact is not possible, the remittance should be handled as outlined under "account payment program," in this section.

7. The on-account payment program may be used to apply exception payments, but this too should require the approval of the credit manager or a company official, unless the customer has specified the type of application verbally (which must be documented) or in writing (as in a remittance advice).

Use of On-Account Payment Program

When customer payments are received without a valid remittance advice, and it is impossible to determine how the payment should be applied and also impossible to contact the customer, it is necessary to have an established procedure for applying the payment to the customer's account.

All on-account payments should be handled as follows:

1. Post the payment on the cash payment journal indicating an on-account payment status.

Figure 21 shows an example of an on-account payment log.

2. List payments on the on-account log as follows:
   A. Account number
   B. Amount
   C. Date applied
   D. Customer check number and date
   E. Customer name
3. All items listed on the on-account log should be followed on a regular basis until the proper application can be verified by the customer. All items in the log should be called at least once a week. At the time verification is established, notations should be made on the log and file adjustment should be made to apply the payment properly.
4. A photocopy of the on-account payment log should be supplied to the credit manager or company management at the end of each month.

Invoice Security

This section describes two aspects of invoice security—the handling and security of blank invoices and the security and maintenance of copies of customer invoices.

All blank invoices should be maintained in a locked cabinet or room that is regulated at all times. All unnumbered invoices should be for use only on the computer, which assigns a number. Any unnumbered invoices that are taken from the controlled area, and used for hand typing, or hand writing a customer invoice must be documented as to the number taken, the customer invoiced, the invoice number used, and other information that might be pertinent to the company operations.

Copies of all customer invoices should be maintained in orderly files. A specific employee should be assigned responsibility for maintaining the integrity of these files.

Figure 21. On-account payment log.

ON-ACCOUNT PAYMENT LOG

DATE	ACCT NO.	NAME	TOTAL AMOUNT REMITED	AMOUNT PUT ON-ACCOUNT	CALLED CUSTOMER	DATE RESOLVED

This section also describes the policy and procedures to be used by all employees to ensure that all invoices and invoice copies are maintained in a safe, orderly manner.

Invoice Security Policy

Anyone wishing to leave the immediate area with a file should secure permission from the department manager or his or her assigned representative. Invoices that are taken from the department should be signed out in accordance with procedures specified in this section.

Release of Invoices Outside the Department

During the normal course of business, it becomes necessary to review various invoices. Invoices may be taken out of the file and reviewed or photocopied in the area with verbal approval of the individual responsible for the file's integrity. When it is necessary to remove an invoice from the department, it should be done in accordance with the procedure given below.

All invoices removed from the department should be handled as follows:

1. The responsible staff member of the department should be notified of the intent to remove the documents.
2. The following information should be logged into the invoice out log:
   A. Date invoice taken
   B. Invoice number
   C. Customer name
   D. Person taking the invoice
   E. Reason
   F. Signature of the person taking the invoice
       Figure 22 shows an example of an invoice out log.

Figure 22. Invoice out log.

Invoice Out Log

Date Out	Invoice Number	Estimated Return Date	Individual	Department	Date Return	Verified By

3. While the invoice is out of the department, it is the full responsibility of the signer.
4. When the documents are returned to the department, the signer should do the following:
   A. Write the date returned in the log
   B. Get the file clerk or another department staff member to sign as a witness to the return of the documents. When invoices are returned verify the numbers.
5. File clerk should refile the invoice.

Chapter 10

CREDIT/ COLLECTION DEPARTMENT MANAGEMENT REPORTS

T HIS SECTION describes the policy and the procedures that are to be followed when analyzing the compliance by credit and collection department management and personnel with general company policies, and company credit and collection policies and procedures.

The credit/collection department should inform company management of the condition of the company's outstanding accounts receivable file. An analysis of all credit/collection activity should be submitted monthly, outlining these functions.

A *Credit/Collection Department Analysis Report* should be submitted to company management no later than the fifteenth of the following month, and should contain figures for the preceding month. The report should be in six sections (outlined in the procedures in this section) and should include back-up material as required by the specific report.

Procedure #1: Credit Application Analysis Report

This report will communicate to company management the number of credit applications received in the current month and year-to-date, and the number accepted, rejected, and pending as of month end.

The credit/collection department should prepare a report of credit application activity and submit it to management as Section I of the Credit/Collection Department Analysis Report.

Procedure #2: Delinquency Analysis Report

This report will communicate to company management the condition of the accounts receivable file with regard to aging. The report will indicate both current month figures and year-to-date figures, with back-up material as specified.

The delinquency analysis report is Section II of the Credit/Collection Department Analysis Report.

The following back-up sheets should be submitted monthly, with the above report:

1. A single sheet indicating the monthly figures shown on the report, in a year-to-date sequence
2. The listing of the accounts with a high-dollar (figure to be determined by company) 90-day delinquency; the following information included:
   A. Account name
   B. Account number
   C. Total delinquency over 90 days
   D. Brief summary of collection activity

Procedure #3: Average Collection Period Report

This report will communicate to company management the average collection period (ACP) for company receivables. The ACP is intended to indicate the average frequency with which company receivables are collected.

The credit/collection department should prepare the information necessary for the report which becomes Section III of the Credit Collection Department Analysis Report.

The figures to be entered are as follows:

1. Year-to-Date Sales: This is the total of all sales, including tax, to date in the current year.
2. Days in the Year: This figure represents the total number of calendar days elapsed in the year as of the report date.
3. Sales per Day: This figure is the figure arrived at by dividing the (1) year-to-date sales by (2) days in the year.
4. Total Outstanding Accounts Receivable As of the Month End: This is the total accounts receivable (open and cash accounts combined) shown on the A/R Files.

224 A PRACTICAL GUIDE TO CREDIT AND COLLECTION

IV Collection Letter Program

	Current Month	Y-T-D
Letters "A" Sent	_____	_____
Letters "B" Sent	_____	_____
COD Letters Sent	_____	_____
Accounts Placed on COD	_____	_____

5. Collection Period: The figure arrived at by dividing (4) total A/R as of month end by (3) sales per day is the collection period. The figure represents days.

Procedure #4: Collection Letter Program Analysis

This section of the Credit/Collection Department Analysis Report gives management the activity in the collection letter program. The number of letter A, letter B, and COD letters, sent to customers is reported (time period to be established by the company), along with the number of accounts placed on COD. This comprises Section IV of the report. An example of the format is shown below.

Procedure #5: Analysis of Attorney/Agency Accounts

This section of the Credit/Collection Department Analysis Report gives management the activity of the accounts that have been turned over to outside collectors for additional collection activity.

The credit/collection department is to submit the information as Section V of the report. An example of the format is shown below:

Procedure #6: Bad Debt Write-Off Analysis

This section of the Credit/Collection Department Analysis Report gives management the bad debt write-off activity.

V   Analysis of Attorney/Agency Accounts

	Current Month	Y-T-D
Accounts Submitted to Outside Collection Services	_____	_____
Dollar Value of Accounts	_____	_____
Accounts Cleared by Outside Collection Services	_____	_____
Total Fees Paid	_____	_____

The report includes the number of accounts written off and the dollar value of these accounts.

The credit/collection department is to submit the information as Section VI of the report. An example of the format is shown below:

VI   Bad Debt Write-Off Analysis

	Current Month	Y-T-D
Total Accounts Written Off	_____	_____
Total Dollar Value	_____	_____
Percent of Dollars Written off to Y-T-D Credit Sales	_____	_____
Percent of Dollars Written off to Total Y-T-D Sales	_____	_____

Chapter 11

DEVELOPING YOUR CREDIT/ COLLECTION PROGRAM

THIS CHAPTER describes the steps that you should take to evaluate your current credit/collection program, and the steps you can take to solve your short-term problems before starting a new program based on the philosophy and procedures explained in this book. If you were to engage me to develop a new program for you, I would take the following steps:

Step 1: Complete the credit and collection department evaluation form as shown in Figures 23 through 25.

Step 2: Define the special handling accounts

Step 3: Pull all invoices and other relevant paperwork for all accounts with items over 90 days old.

Step 4: Determine which accounts are to receive personal direct action within the next two weeks.

Step 5: Send a statement of account to all accounts with a cover letter explaining my action, and what I want from the customer.

Each step has a specific purpose, so I'll explain the program in detail.

Step #1: Complete the Credit/Collection Department Program Evaluation Form

Figure 23 is an example of page 1 of a credit/collection department program evaluation form. I originally designed this form to be used as an in-depth analysis tool for client company's credit/collection department.

I will go through the form section by section and explain how I use the information. There are some questions that I would use to familiarize myself with the company organization and general procedures. I have left these in the form so that a new person with your company can use the checklist to familiarize himself or herself with your company's credit/collection program.

General Information and Organization

You can use this section to gather some general purpose information. If you are new to the company, or new in the department, this will help you get acquainted.

Figure 23. Credit/collection department program analysis form (page 1).

Credit/Collection   Department
Program   Analysis   Form

Company Name _____

Product/Service _____

Target Market _____

    Consumer: _____ Commercial: _____ Government: _____ Special Handling: _____

Organization

Credit/Collection Assigned to: _____

Reports to: _____ Title: _____

Number of Dept. Employees: _____

Does Dept. Have Procedures Manual | Y | N | Are There Written/Verbal Guidelines | Y | N |

Credit Checking

Normal Terms _____ Special Terms _____ Discount _____

Who Completes Credit Application _____

Where _____ Do Cr. Dept. People Interview _____

Primary Source Of Credit History _____

Any Direct Checking Done _____ What Type _____

On All Applications _____ Credit Hist. Eval. Done By_____

Is Each Order Credit Checked _____ Guidelines Established _____ Written ____ Verbal _____

Is There an Approval Pyramid _____

Name	Dollar Limit	Name	Dollar Limit
_____	_____	_____	_____
_____	_____	_____	_____

Does the Company Issue Credit Limits to Customers _____

Levels $ _____ $ _____ $ _____ $ _____

Is There an "Approaching Limit" Flagging System _____

What Is the Procedure for Re-Evaluating Credit Limits _____

_____

_____

PRODUCT/SERVICE. What is the company's product or service? Question the people in the credit/collection (C/C) department and then ask some of the sales representatives the same questions. You may find that they have different answers.

TARGET MARKET. What is the target market? In other words, who are the prospective customers?

What percent of the customer base is . . .

Consumer   ———
Commercial   ———
Special Handling   ———

I use this as a gauge of the general type of collection program that the company will need. For instance, if the accounts receivable file is made up of just consumers, I know this means that there are no special handling accounts, and that all customers will receive the same notices, letters, and collection calls.

In companies that deal with commercial accounts there are generally some special handling accounts. This information can give you a feel for the amount of special handling activities that are required.

CREDIT/COLLECTION FUNCTION ASSIGNED TO. Who is the person responsible for the C/C program? In a small company this may be the name of the person who is responsible for all C/C activity. In a larger company it would be the manager of the department.

REPORTS TO. Who does the person responsible for the C/C program report to? Give the name and the title. This can give you a clue as to the importance the company places on the program, and the way in which the department runs.

For instance, there could be a different emphasis on the department if the manager reported to the vice-president of finance rather than the sales manager. I have known companies that had the C/C department under the sales manager rather than a finance department executive. It takes a well-rounded sales executive to be able to oversee both the sales activity and the C/C department. I always want to see how the company views the C/C activity, and I use the reporting structure as one indicator.

TITLE. What is the person's title? I have come to realize that titles within companies are extremely important, and therefore, the C/C department manager's title gives a clue to the importance your company places in the C/C activity.

For example, if the sales department is headed by a vice-president and the C/C function is headed by a person with the title "manager," there could be an imbalance in the status of decisions made by the C/C department. This might influence the way that many "borderline" credit decisions go. The titles given to the head of the sales department and the head of the C/C department. This can give you another clue as to how the C/C function is seen by the company as a whole.

NUMBER OF DEPARTMENT EMPLOYEES. This is just a gauge of size. When you start doing the work load analysis, you rate the total number of collectors required with the total number employed.

DOES DEPARTMENT HAVE PROCEDURES MANUAL? If you do not have a manual, you can use Chapters 7 through 10 as the basis for developing one.

ARE THERE WRITTEN/VERBAL GUIDELINES?

> In addition to a manual   ———
> In place of a manual   ———
> Written   ———
> Verbal   ———

Credit Checking

This information can give you a good feel for the level of credit checking that your company performs. If you find

weak points in the process, note them and after you have
completed this evaluation, reread Chapters 4 and 7, and
make recommendations to your company management about
the changes you feel are needed.

NORMAL TERMS. Normal credit terms are net 30 days. If
your company has different terms you should be aware of
this when contacting past due customers. To design a collection notice and letter program you must know the credit
terms that the company extends.

SPECIAL TERMS. Are there any special terms given? Are
they given to all customers, or are there special customers
that receive special terms? How and why are special terms
given?

You must be aware of all "special" payment plans that
might be available (whether formal or informal). Are there
regular special plans that are given to customers as part of
special promotions or incentive plans? Find out about all
exception payment plans. You need to know if the accounts
receivable aging program takes these special payment programs into account when your monthly aging is run.

DISCOUNTS. Many companies have discount programs. You
need to know how and why they are given. You must know
how discounts are handled. Does the total of the invoice
reflect the discount? If not, how can you know if there is
a discount on invoices. The most common discounts given
are for fast payments. Two percent for payment within 10
days of invoice, for example. You need to know if the
company sticks strictly to this policy. Are there customers
who might be allowed to take discounts beyond the normal
discount terms? If so, who are they and what is the rule?

CREDIT APPLICATION FORMAT ADEQUATE . . . WHY?
Do you feel that the credit application provides all the
customer information that you need to perform an adequate
credit check? If not, give the areas you would add or change

and state why. After you have completed this audit you can then make formal recommendations to management to change the credit application format.

WHO COMPLETES CREDIT APPLICATION? Does the customer complete the credit application, or perhaps the sales representative completes the form, or it may be someone in your department. Is it in person, or over the phone?

WHERE? Where is the application completed? In your office? At the customer's office? Or perhaps, some other place? Find out where the application is completed.

DO CREDIT DEPARTMENT PEOPLE INTERVIEW? If you have a chance to interview applicants, it gives you a better "feel" for the applicant. This gives you a chance to ask additional questions and jot notes on the application, which you may want to refer to if the account becomes delinquent. If you do interview and fill out credit applications, you should start reading about body language and other books on human psychology.

PRIMARY SOURCE OF CREDIT HISTORY. Does your company use a credit bureau? If not, how is the information gathered? Are additional steps needed to strengthen the credit information gathering process? If so, what are they?

ANY DIRECT CHECKING DONE? Do you call other companies in the area to help gather information for the credit decision? Is this the only means of credit information? If so, is there a credit bureau that you can use to augment the information gathering process? Keep in mind that a credit applicant will only give you the best references. It is bad business to make decisions with only half of the relevant data available.

WHAT TYPE? If you do direct checking, what is the method? What questions do you ask? Can you "upgrade" the process? If so, how and would it be worthwhile? Why?

ON ALL APPLICATIONS? Are all applications direct checked? If so, why are all applications checked using the most expensive method? Is there a valid reason? You may not have a credit bureau in your area, or you may have one that doesn't keep up-to-date files. This would be a valid reason for using the direct checking method. If you have a credit bureau that keeps up-to-date records, you should reconsider your credit checking procedures if you direct check every account. Direct checking is expensive when you consider the personal time it takes.

CREDIT HISTORY EVALUATION DONE BY . . .. Who evaluates the credit information and makes the final decision to accept or reject the application? Is it the credit manager? A clerk with no credit industry background? A sales representative? Maybe it's you.

IS EACH ORDER CREDIT CHECKED? Are all credit orders, from established customers and new customers alike, given a credit check? Established customers should be checked for past due invoices and the dollars outstanding if you use credit limits. All customers should be given a credit check before accepting new orders.

GUIDELINES ESTABLISHED? There should be an established procedure for clearing all credit orders. It could be that your established customers are creating new invoices faster than you can clean up the old ones. If this is a problem for you, talk it over with your management, and with the sales department if necessary, and set up a standard procedure for handling credit orders.

WRITTEN OR VERBAL? If you have verbal guidelines, but they are not being adhered to, make them into written procedures that require a credit check of current billing before an order can be accepted. I do not advocate written procedures just for the sake of having them. But if this area is a problem, you should most certainly establish an order checking procedure, verbal or written.

IS THERE AN APPROVAL PYRAMID? Are there credit approval limits within the company? If so, list the dollar amounts and the name of the manager(s) or officer(s) that can approve the amount.

You need to know this information if you are part of the credit gathering and approval process.

DOES THE COMPANY ISSUE CREDIT LIMITS? Does your company issue credit limits to your customers. If so, list the limits and a criteria that may be used to determine the limit.

IS THERE AN "APPROACHING LIMIT" FLAGGING SYS-TEM? You should be able to tell when a customer is close to his or her credit limit. If your company doesn't have a mechanism for doing this, you should establish one. This is a good time to put your computer to work. A system that gives you up-to-date customer account totals and credit limits is done easier by computer than human.

WHAT IS THE PROCEDURE FOR REEVALUATING CREDIT LIMITS? Find out what the procedure is for raising and lowering credit limits. Hopefully it is more sophisticated than "the customer needs to buy more product." You should have some type of time period within the current limit before it is raised. If a customer wants a credit limit that is much higher than the current one, you may want to do an entirely new investigation.

If you do not have a procedure, review the procedure for reevaluating credit limits in Chapter 7.

File Maintenance Program

Figure 24 shows page 2 of the program evaluation form. This review of your file maintenance program will help you

Figure 24. Credit/collection department program analysis form (page 2).

File Maintenance   Page 2

Credits Open _____ Applied _____ Credits Current _____ Aged ____

Unapplied Cash Current _____ Aged _____ Over/Short Pmt Current _____ Aged____

Open Credits _____ # "On-Account" Pmts _____ # Over/Short Pmts _____

Small Balance W/O Program in Effect _____ Adequate Cr/Db Memo Program _____

Overall File Maintenance Program Rating _____

_____

_____

Collection Program

Does Sales Get Involved _____ Are Statements Sent Regularly _____

Notices Who Gets Them _____ Schedule _____

Is a Record Kept _____ How _____

Letters Who Get Them _____ Schedule _____

Is a Record Kept _____ How _____

Telephone Who is Called _____

Is a Priority Schedule Used _____ What _____

A Record Kept _____ How _____

_____

Personal Who Makes Them _____
Visits Who Gets Them _____

Purpose _____

Record Kept _____ How _____

Outside Name of Service _____
Collection Who Assigns _____When _____
Service How Followed _____

Criteria for Bad Debt W/O _____

_____

	Total YTD	Total Dollars	Total Collected	Percent of YTD Sales
Attorney/Agency Accounts				
Written off to Bad Debt				

determine the integrity of your accounts receivable delinquency figures.

CREDITS OPEN OR APPLIED. This is the total amount of credits that are *open* and the amount of those that are issued against specific invoice numbers. This tells you the total amount of open credits that have been applied to specific open invoices.

When you give credit for erroneous billing, returned merchandise, or for any valid reason, the amount should offset the total invoiced amount. When this is done, it is valid for the credit to age with the invoice.

CREDITS CURRENT OR AGED? Open credits that are not issued against an open invoice should not be aged. All unapplied credits should remain in the current column. This reduces the value of the current column and artificially raises the delinquency percentages. This means that the collector has an incentive to get the credits resolved and off the accounts receivable file. If the customer won't use the credit, issue a refund check.

UNAPPLIED CASH CURRENT OR AGED? This category is the same as credit memos. This type of payment should remain in the current column and must be resolved with the customer as soon as possible. Any customer payments that cannot be resolved at time of application should be followed until the customer determines how the payment should be applied.

If you have a large number of on-account payments on your accounts receivable file, review Chapter 9. There is a complete procedure given for handling on-account payments.

NUMBER OF OVERS AND SHORTS. You must attempt to resolve a payment that does not match the exact amount of the invoice it is meant to pay. There are many reasons for customers paying invoices over or short the invoice amount. If you have this type of problem, review the "Cash Application" section of Chapter 9.

NUMBER OF OPEN CREDITS. If your file has a large number of open credits that are not linked to an open invoice, you need to take a close look at your credit memo procedures. You also need to try to find if there is a single reason for the credits. It may be that another area of the company is creating unnecessary work for you and the person that must issue the credit memo.

When a credit memo is issued, and it is against an invoice that has been paid, a copy of the credit memo should be sent to the customer, asking that the credit be used as soon as possible. If the credit is not used on the next payment, send a letter to the customer asking how they want the credit handled.

A simple form letter can be used with two boxes to be checked.

- Issue a refund check
- Use the credit against invoice #—

State clearly that you will issue a refund check if the matter is not resolved by (give a specific date).

NUMBER OF ON-ACCOUNT PAYMENTS. When a payment is received, you must attempt to apply it as specified on the remittance advice. If the customer does not include a remittance advice, and you cannot easily tell how the payment is to be applied, you may want to apply the total check as an on-account payment. If you do this, you must have a procedure for following the situation with the customer until it is resolved.

If you have a large number of on-account payments on your A/R file, review Chapter 9. There is a complete procedure given for handling on-account payments.

NUMBER OF OVER/SHORT PAYMENTS. Handle these in the same manner as on-account payments.

IS A SMALL BALANCE WRITE-OFF PROGRAM IN EFFECT? You should have an amount that your company management has defined as a small balance write-off candidate. This amount might be $1, or it might be as high as $5. Whatever the amount, you should have an easy procedure for clearing a balance that is not worth attempting to resolve with the customer.

You may have a program on your computer (if you have one) that reads the entire open account file and flags (or deletes) accounts and/or invoices that have a balance owing that is less than your small balance amount.

If this write-off is processed with an automatic computer program, the program must print a "Small Balance Write-off Report" that shows the invoices that were written off. It is very important that you have an audit trail to trace back through, and a listing that your accounting department (even if that is you) can use to trace the debits and credits issued to the general ledger accounts.

If your computer program(s) is not linked directly to your company's general ledger, you will have to give the accounting department a copy of the "Small Balance Write-off Report" each time you run the program so it can make the appropriate entries in the general ledger.

ADEQUATE CREDIT/DEBIT MEMO PROGRAM? If you find a large percent of open credit or debit memos in your file, you should investigate the procedure used to issue them. If there is a large number open, it may be that the customer is not getting a copy and therefore never applies them to open items.

Thoroughly investigate your credit/debit memo program to be sure that it is being properly administered, not just appearing to run smoothly because nothing is being done.

Collection Program

This section of the analysis form helps find potential weak spots in your collection program. You can use the information gathered in this section to evaluate your current program and compare it to the program presented in this book.

DOES SALES GET INVOLVED? In some companies the sales representatives are responsible for delinquent account collections in some form. Some account representatives do all the collections, while other companies do not want their salespeople involved with delinquent accounts. If the sales rep is on a commission, and is charged back for unpaid accounts, it makes sense for the rep to participate, or have a chance to participate in the collection cycle.

I have found that account reps make very good collectors, because it is really *their money* that is being collected. If your company has commissioned salespeople, and they are not currently part of the collection cycle, you may want to ask if they want to participate.

ARE STATEMENTS SENT REGULARLY? Does your company send monthly statements, or a monthly billing document of some type to your customer? If you do, the statement (or other document) can be used as the first past due notice.

If your company sells merchandise or service on an open account basis, where customers buy products throughout the month, you should be sending a monthly statement. The statement will let the customer's accounts payable department know if they have received all invoice activity for the month.

Most businesses do not pay from a statement, but they do like to check all activity from the last statement.

If your company sends out statements, are they indeed being sent out regularly, and on a timely basis?

NOTICES AND LETTERS. The notice program is very important because if it is carefully planned and executed, it will prompt many slow payers to send in their money without further contact. The notice program lets your accounts know that they have passed the normal, agreed upon payment period. In many cases something has happened to cause them to forget or overlook sending the payment. This program is only good for this type of account. But if it is automated, and can be sent out to everyone with very little extra work, do it.

Define who gets notices, what the schedule is for sending them, and if a record is kept, define the method. This gives you a concise definition of the current status of the delinquent notice program.

When you start defining the notice program you may find that you need to expand the program. But if you find that you are spending far too much time deciding who should get a notice, and when they need to be mailed, you may find that you want to cut back on the program and use it strictly as a first contact for your "letter program," or low-dollar delinquent accounts.

The collection letter program should be used for the low-dollar delinquent account. There are two types of low-dollar accounts that receive these letters.

The first includes accounts whose dollar value causes them to fall below your telephone collection program. These accounts will receive only collection letters. The second type of account is the bottom half of your "telephone collection" program call list. These accounts are to be called later in the month, and therefore should receive a letter before the call.

Define who gets the collection letters, what the schedule is for sending them. If a record is kept, define the method. This gives you a concise definition of the current status of the delinquent collection letter program.

TELEPHONE PROGRAM. The telephone collection program should be the backbone of your collection effort. You should be collecting the big dollar accounts, and therefore collecting most of your delinquent money using this method. This is what it should be—now document the way it is.

Define who is called, if the calls are prioritized, and, if so, the rationale used. If a record of each call is kept, define the method used to follow the telephone collection activity.

PERSONAL VISITS. Personal visits to customers should be kept to a minimum. There are only two reasons to make a personal visit—special circumstances that require an "in person" collection call and a public relations call to large, high-volume accounts. Now define your reasons for making personal visits.

Define who makes the calls. Perhaps it is the sales representative, or a member of management—or it might be you. It should not be a beginner in the department.

Now define who gets personal attention and the purpose of the calls. If a record is kept, write down the method of record keeping.

OUTSIDE SERVICE. An outside collection service should be used by almost everyone. The only types of business that I can think of that would not use an outside service would be attorneys and/or companies that are owned or managed by a member of the bar.

If you have an outside collection service, write down who it is, who assigns the accounts, the time in the collection program (days, months, or whatever time period) they are assigned, and how they are followed. Now fill in the dollars for:

> Total accounts assigned YTD
> Total dollars assigned YTD
> Total dollars collected YTD
> Percent of YTD sales represented by
>   the dollars assigned

If you have used, or currently are using more than one outside service, fill in the numbers for all outside services used.

CRITERIA FOR WRITE-OFF. Define the criteria for a bad debt write-off at your company. If you do not have written criteria, you should seriously consider writing one. Now write in the amounts for:

- Total number of bad debt write-offs for the current year
- Total dollars written off
- Total dollars recovered from previously written-off accounts
- Percent of total sales represented by bad debt write-offs

Now you can see the effect of your collection efforts. You will also have one concrete measurement to judge your new collection program against the old one.

The areas you have just analyzed in your current collection program are the areas you should study carefully when you start building your new program. These statements and dollar figures give you a good overview of what you are now doing and the results you are achieving. Consider each carefully as you define your new program.

Delinquency Analysis

Figure 25 shows page 3 of the program evaluation form.

Your current delinquency analysis gives a snapshot of how well your program is working. If I were to analyze your program, I would go back at least six months and work up the delinquency figures for each month. If this is something that you do regularly, you are just that much ahead of the game.

As I define what you should be looking at, think seriously about developing a six month history for all of these figures. It will give you the trend of your effectiveness, not just a single snapshot of the current month's effectiveness.

NUMBER OF ACCOUNTS. Write in the total number of accounts in your A/R file.

TOTAL DOLLAR VALUE. Write in the total value of your accounts receivable file.

Figure 25. Credit/collection department program analysis form (page 3).

Delinquency Analysis

Approxiate Number of Accounts _____ Total Dollar Value $ _____

Delinquency:

	Current			30-day			60-day			90-day			6-month			Total	
$	#	%	$	#	%	$	#	%	$	#	%	$	#	%	$	#	%

LARGE ACCOUNT ANALYSIS:

	Dollars Outstanding	Number of Accounts
Top 10%		
Top 20%		
Top 30%		
Top 40%		

COLLECTION DAYS OUTSTANDING:

$$\frac{\text{YTD Sales } \$ \underline{\hspace{3cm}}}{\text{No. of Days}} = \$ \underline{\hspace{3cm}} \text{ Sales per Day}$$

$$\frac{\text{Total A/R Outstanding } \$ \underline{\hspace{2cm}}}{\text{Salaes per Day}} = \underline{\hspace{2cm}} \text{ Days}$$

Workload Analysis

Total No. of Accounts _____ No. of Collectors _____ Accts/Coll _____

Types of Accounts	Single Item	2 - 10 Items	10+ Items	Lg. Accounts

Number
Percent

Top 20% General Condition _____

_____

Other Duties Assigned to Collectors _____

_____

Number of Major Accounts _____ Dollar Value $ _____

Percent of Total Accounts _____ % Dollar Value _____ %

Telephone Calls Needed per Month _____ Time Available _____ Labor Hrs.

Number of Calls That Can be Made _____ Adequate _____

Number of Collectors Needed _____ Reason _____

_____

_____

DELINQUENCY. Spread your delinquency by the normal accounting periods shown. Use the grid shown on the analysis form to spread your delinquency trend. It will help you get a better picture of your delinquency trend if you list the last 6 months delinquency figures. If you just put down the figures for the current month, you have a snapshot of

your current delinquency, but if you list 6 months or longer
you get an indication of the way the trend is moving.

The 90-day figure includes all accounts 90-days and
over—this includes the 6-month accounts. The 6-month
number gives you a feel for the total amount in the 90-
day column that is not collectible. After 6 months you have
little chance of collecting, unless payment has been withheld
for administrative reasons such as bad invoice amounts, no
purchase orders included on invoices, or other similar reasons.

LARGE ACCOUNT ANALYSIS. This ranking gives you a
feeling for the impact that large accounts have on your
collection program. You may find that you don't have any
accounts that are large enough to make any impact. If this
is the case, you have your answer—none.

But most companies do have certain large accounts
that cause a higher than normal amount of their outstanding
accounts receivable total.

Step 1. Go back to the first two totals in this section—
"number of accounts" and "total dollar value."
Divide the total dollar value by the number of
accounts and you have the average account
balance.

Step 2. Rank your account totals for accounts that are
greater than the average balance. Keep a running total so that you will know when you have
reached 10 percent of the total outstanding,
20 percent, and so on.

This exercise will be very enlightening if you have
never thought of your accounts in this type of priority
ranking before. You will most likely find that a very high
percentage of your total outstanding accounts receivable is
wrapped up in a minority of accounts.

The point here is to find out if you have been giving all of the delinquent dollars outstanding an equal collection effort. If you have 5 percent of your total accounts making up 30 or 40 percent of your delinquent dollars, and you have been giving each account the same collection effort, you have been wasting some of your time.

AN EXAMPLE. The following example gives you an idea of the concept:

Fact 1: You have $80,000, 30 days or older, in your accounts receivable file.

Fact 2: This money is distributed in one hundred accounts—which gives you an $800 average account balance.

Fact 3: As you add up the accounts by highest total outstanding first, you find that the five largest accounts total $16,000. This means that 5 percent of your accounts make up 20 percent of your total delinquency.

WORK LOAD ANALYSIS. This section will help you get an understanding of the number of collectors that are required to collect the type and number of accounts that your company has.

ACCOUNTS PER COLLECTOR. Enter the total number of accounts divided by the number of collectors to get the accounts/collector. This figure is the average number of accounts that each collector handles.

TYPES OF ACCOUNTS. This data tells you the types of accounts that you have. These accounts are broken down into "single item," "2–10 items," "10-plus items," and "large accounts." You may want to devise your own criteria for listing accounts that will make better sense for your circumstances. That's fine, this is only a guideline. The idea here is to find out how your accounts break down from a work load basis.

AN EXAMPLE. If you have 1000 accounts and five collectors, this means that each collector has an average of 200 accounts to follow. This seems like a good method for dividing your accounts among the collectors.

But wait a minute, after you analyze your accounts by number of outstanding items, you will most likely find that some accounts have few line items, while others may have pages of open line items.

If your company has a diversity in the number of line items per account, it is far more equitable to assign work load based on line items than on accounts.

TOP 20 PERCENT. List the number of major accounts that you have and the dollar value. Then list the percent of the total A/R file for both of these figures.

These figures can come from the "large account analysis" that you just finished in the last section. "Top 20 percent" is an arbitrary figure that you may want to change to fit your circumstances.

GENERAL CONDITION. Write an analysis of the general condition of the A/R file and the collection program. Refer to the material in this book as a basis for your analysis.

This will help you determine whether the "normal" line item per collector is adequate for your circumstances. The worse the condition of the file, the lower the line item per collector.

OTHER DUTIES ASSIGNED TO COLLECTORS. This is a big factor to consider when assigning the work load. Determine exactly how many hours the person is working as a collector and assign the collection work load proportionately. Some of the "other duties" that might be assigned are the resolution of outstanding credits/debits, general file maintenance, and the like. These additional tasks will be more time consuming in the large accounts, if the file maintenance work has not been kept current.

TELEPHONE CALLS NEEDED PER MONTH. It would be easy to say that one call is required for each open account with at least one delinquent item—it would be easy but not very effective.

To determine the number of calls needed you must calculate the number of accounts that meets the criteria for your telephone collection program. Now of these accounts, how many have multiple line items, and how do they break down?

You will need at least one call for every account in your collection program. The multiple line accounts may require more than one call per month. But how many? A good rule of thumb is to assign one call for every ten line items. So, for an account with thirty line items, you can allow the collector three calls. This is in addition to the time assigned for file maintenance.

In a normal small or medium-size business, where the A/R file is clean and there are no hidden time-consuming traps, each full-time collector should be able to handle between 750 and 900 accounts.

It breaks down like this:

In an 8-hour day a person can be effective for 7 hours. This means that there are 420 minutes of effective work. A collector should be able to make one call every 10 minutes, which means they should be able to call about 40 accounts per day.

There are 22 workdays in a month, therefore they should be able to make 880 calls per month.

Full-time collectors with no responsibilities other than telephone collections can handle up to 900 accounts.

Collectors who must handle credit applications, post customer accounts, handle problem accounts and billing discrepancies, or handle file maintenance, would have their ability to call greatly reduced.

Use the following guideline when you assess the work load for your department:

1. "Single item" accounts, such as, time payment, revolving charge, rental or lease billing payments can be called at the rate of 40 to 50 calls each day. Seventy-five percent of these calls will be completed, which means that 750 to 900 effective calls per month can be made by a collector (with no other responsibility assigned) working this type of account.
2. Commercial accounts with 2 to 10 items or transactions per month, can be called at the rate of 35 to 40 calls each day with the same 75 percent effectiveness factor. This means a collector assigned the responsibility for calling (and only calling) accounts can handle 500 to 600 accounts monthly.
3. Accounts with over 10 transactions per month greatly reduce the number of calls a collector can handle.
4. Additional duties will also reduce the number of calls a collector can make. A time study should be done (see Figure 20) to determine exactly how much time is available for telephone collection activity.

A parameter can now be established for the top dollar limit in the collection letter program using the following information:

1. The lowest dollar figure of the "top 20 percent accounts"
2. The results of the time study that will reveal the amount of time available for the collector to make telephone calls

The number of top 20 percent accounts will tell you how many telephone calls should be made each month. The results of the time study will indicate how many telephone collection calls the collection department can make. These two figures will allow a parameter to be established for the top dollar limit of the collection letter program, and the bottom dollar limit for the telephone collection program.

TIME AVAILABLE IN LABOR HOURS. Now that you have a basis for calculating the number of calls you *need* each month, calculate the number of calls that the people in your department *can make* each month. Is this adequate?

NUMBER OF COLLECTORS NEEDED. When you know how many calls you need, you can calculate the number of collectors you need to handle the work load. If your figures don't fit the guidelines shown, give your reasons for differing.

Now you have some down-to-earth, real-world figures to show your boss why you need all those additional people.

SUMMARY. The areas of your credit and collection program that are covered in this analysis form give you a good picture of the way things are now. Use this information to compare what you have learned while reading this book with the way you now administer your credit and collection program.

If you need specific procedures, refer to Chapters 7, 8, 9, and 10, and use the written procedure as a guideline for your new procedures. These chapters can be used as is, but I think that your situation is probably too unique to simply take the procedures as written and *adopt them* to your company's other written and verbal procedures. It would make more sense for you to *adapt them* to your unique environment.

Step #2: Define the Special Handling Accounts

You have already done the research for this step. Now you need to determine which of the accounts that fit into your top 20 percent on the analysis sheet are true special handling accounts. You may have accounts that fit this category now because they have not been worked.

Go back over the last three or four months billing and determine the accounts that have a large volume of invoices, or have high-balance invoices—on a regular basis. These accounts will become your special handling accounts that you call every month, and with whom you will build a good rapport.

Step #3: Pull All Relevant Paperwork

Every account that has any line items over 90 days delinquent should become a short-term special handling account. Pull the appropriate paperwork for all open items for these accounts and photocopy these source documents.

This may be a major project if your accounts receivable file has not been administered properly until now. If the task is more than you can handle within a month, ask your management for some short-term temporary help. It will pay off in the long run. You will most likely collect enough of the delinquent money to pay for the temporary help.

If the job is too much of an undertaking to even consider doing within a month's time, prioritize the accounts into the oldest, and the largest, and work the program from that direction.

I was once given an assignment to clean up an office that had never been worked properly, and when I took it over no one had even sat at the desk to open the mail for two months. I started working the program as I have explained it here and within a year the office was within the corporation guidelines for delinquency. While a year may seem like a long time, the company knew that the situation was bad and had given me two years to clean it up.

Step #4: Determine Direct Action Accounts

The next step is to determine which accounts are going to receive your direct action now. You are now armed with source documents and you can call the large, old accounts and give PO numbers, work order numbers, time and date of delivery, or whatever the customer requires to pay the billing.

Step #5: Send Out Statements With Cover Letter

If I was doing the job, I would send a statement to each customer with a copy of the backup, source documents for each of the outstanding items.

Even if I planned to call the accounts, I would send them this documentation with a cover letter first. This gives the customer a chance to read over the letter and research the delinquent items before you call.

I would also handwrite a short message such as, "I will call you next Wednesday, the seventeenth, to discuss these outstanding items." This is a nice touch that will show the customer that you took time to send a personal message.

Summary

The five steps explained above are the very first things you must do to start your program. This is the action that you must use to turn the tide of delinquency and put the credit and collection program on a strong footing.

After you have taken the short-term steps to collect the old invoices, you must also set down a relevant program for the long term and start sending out notices and letters, and making collection calls on a regular basis to the accounts that fall into your telephone collection program.

If you establish a credit and collection program as I have outlined in this book, you will soon be making calls to current accounts, "just to make sure that the billing is correct and the invoice will be paid this month."

I have used the program in a number of situations and it has always worked. I once used it in a situation where I worked myself out of a job. There simply wasn't enough work in the accounts that I had been assigned for management to justify keeping me in that position—so they promoted me.

Good luck with your new program. I would really be interested in hearing how your program worked both in the short term and the long term. You can write to me in care of the publisher.

INDEX

255